A Brief Primer of
Helping Skills

A Brief Primer of
Helping Skills

Jeffrey A. Kottler
California State University, Fullerton

SAGE Publications
Los Angeles • London • New Delhi • Singapore

For information:

Sage Publications, Inc.
2455 Teller Road
Thousand Oaks,
   California 91320
E-mail: order@sagepub.com

Sage Publications India Pvt. Ltd.
B 1/I 1 Mohan Cooperative
   Industrial Area
Mathura Road, New Delhi 110 044
India

Sage Publications Ltd.
1 Oliver's Yard
55 City Road
London EC1Y 1SP
United Kingdom

Sage Publications Asia-Pacific Pte. Ltd.
33 Pekin Street #02-01
Far East Square
Singapore 048763

Printed in the United States of America

Library of Congress Cataloging-in-Publication Data

Kottler, Jeffrey A.
A brief primer of helping skills/Jeffrey A. Kottler.
    p. cm.
Includes bibliographical references and index.
ISBN 978-1-4129-5922-3 (cloth)
ISBN 978-1-4129-5923-0 (pbk.)
   1. Counseling. 2. Psychotherapy. 3. Helping behavior. I. Title.

BF636.6.K68 2008
158′.3—dc22   2007020492

This book is printed on acid-free paper.

14   15   16   17   18   10   9   8   7   6   5   4   3   2

Acquisitions Editor:	Kassie Graves
Editorial Assistant:	Veronica Novak
Production Editor:	Libby Larson
Copy Editor:	Julie Gwin
Typesetter:	C&M Digitals (P) Ltd.
Proofreader:	Theresa Kay
Indexer:	Michael Ferreira
Cover Designer:	Candice Harman
Marketing Manager:	Carmel Withers

Contents

Preface

There is something incongruent about the very idea of a primer for basic helping. After all, we are talking about a discipline that, although held together by a specific body of research, a set of theoretical assumptions, and a collection of skills and interventions, is incredibly complicated and requires years of intensive training to master. Nevertheless, the act of helping people deal with problems of daily living is an enterprise that takes place, both formally and informally, every day by a wide variety of professionals. Although much of this therapeutic work is undertaken by mental health specialists in psychology, counseling, social work, psychiatry, psychiatric nursing, and family therapy, others in education, medicine, human services, law, public policy, health, nursing, the clergy, and business also engage in helping efforts. Even with a basic introduction to the skills of helping, it is possible not only to significantly improve professional effectiveness but also enhance all personal relationships.

Purpose of This Book

This book is intended to give students in various professions a basic overview of the theory, process, and skills of helping methods. It is designed as a resource and operating manual for those in human service professions to learn the basics involved in developing helping relationships, assessing and diagnosing complaints, promoting exploration and understanding, and designing and implementing action plans. It covers the foundational theory, core skills, and standard interventions used when helping others work through personal struggles.

This text is intended as a primary and secondary text in both undergraduate and graduate courses in counseling, psychology, human services, social work, education, family studies, marital and family therapy, pastoral work, nursing, human resource development, and other helping professions. It may also be used as a supplementary text for allied health and professional fields such as law, medicine, communications, and others.

State of the Field

Mental health and human service programs have changed dramatically in the past decades. Managed care, innovations in research, integrative theory, multicultural lenses, and new paradigms have revolutionized what social workers, therapists, counselors, and human service workers do. No longer are "active listening" and other basic skills enough. Nowadays, helpers must not only be expected to make a difference in a rather short period of time, often in a few sessions or less, but they must also demonstrate that what they do is effective.

A Brief Primer of Helping Skills is intended to be a practical book, encouraging you to address the realities of helping people and to get started applying what you learn immediately. It is assumed that other courses and training experiences will supplement this brief introduction, giving you an in-depth study of the research and theoretical base for the ideas presented here. Because of space limitations, at the end of each chapter, I have suggested other sources you might consult. I have also included both reflective and practice activities that you can use to personalize the material and apply the concepts to your work and life.

The present text integrates the basic theory and research in the fields of counseling, social work, psychology, education, family therapy, pastoral counseling, and other helping professions into a unified model of intervention. Although there is much debate and many disagreements among various helping professionals about the best way to promote change, I have tried to reconcile some discrepancies, synthesize much of the theory, and integrate several strategies from a broad range of disciplines. The result is a generic approach to helping people that includes those core skills and interventions that most practitioners use in their jobs, regardless of their work settings and personal preferences.

Overview of Contents

The first chapter sets the scene for what follows by talking frankly about the best ways to help people. This advice will encourage you to approach the subject with an active frame of mind, committed to personalizing the concepts in your own life and applying the ideas to your work. This is not the sort of content that can be learned from reading a book unless you are prepared to practice the skills consistently. That is why it is imperative to complete the activities at the end of each chapter; otherwise, the concepts and strategies you read about will never really become part of your interpersonal style.

Chapter 2 covers the major theoretical approaches that form the foundation for helping. This brief survey will introduce you to the basic language and concepts that are employed by practitioners. Your goal, this early in your training, is not to understand all the nuances that make one approach different from others, but rather to grasp the idea that there are many alternative ways of helping people, each of which emphasizes special features of human experience. This book will combine the best parts of each theory into an integrated model.

Chapter 3 reviews the process of helping as it often unfolds in sessions. There are progressive stages that are somewhat universal across settings, theories, and even cultures. Regardless of how you propose to help someone, you must initially find out what is going on, then explore the problem and its context. Finally, based on what you have learned, you implement some sort of intervention.

Consistent with the generic approach to helping, Chapter 4 discusses the nature of the relationships you will construct with people you help. Although the specific kind of alliance will be forged according to the person's complaints, needs, and cultural background, as well as your own work setting and style, certain universal principles will be reviewed.

In Chapter 5, we get to the real nuts and bolts of establishing rapport, conducting an assessment, formulating a diagnosis, and fostering a degree of insight into the problem. This leads, quite naturally, to the action phase described in Chapter 6. The core strategies involved in exploring and resolving problems are described and illustrated with sufficient detail to enable you to make them part of your repertoire.

Contemporary practice now requires us to function much more efficiently than we could have ever imagined a decade ago. Chapter 7 teaches you the basics involved in planning and implementing brief interventions—those designed to work in just a few sessions. Chapter 8 examines how you can use the skills you learned in various group structures, a modality that is particularly responsive to client needs and organizational realities.

In Chapter 9, the book closes by helping you look at the consequences of being a helper, both personally and professionally. You will be encouraged to apply what you have learned to your own life, making you a more powerful model of what you wish to teach to others.

Although necessarily limited in scope and depth, this brief overview of helping will get you started in your service to others. The process of learning these concepts and skills requires your active involvement in the process. This means not merely attending class and reading the text, but challenging yourself to personalize the content as much as possible, as well as applying the material to your work and life.

Acknowledgments

I am grateful for the thoughtful and constructive feedback of the following reviewers, who read an earlier draft of the manuscript and made many helpful suggestions that were incorporated into the present volume:

Jennifer Crissman Ishler, *The Pennsylvania State University*
Victoria T. Grando, *Arizona State University*
Laura Hensley Choate, *Louisiana State University*
Russell Lee, *Bemidji State University*
Michael J. Mason, *Villanova University*
Fernando F. Padró, *Monmouth University*
Eileen M. Russo, *University of Bridgeport*
Colin C. Ward, *Oakland University*
Lia Willis, *Columbia College*

I would also like to thank my editors, Kassie Graves and Julie Gwin, for their help conceptualizing a primer that covers the most important concepts in an accessible format.

Jeffrey A. Kottler
Fullerton, California

1

Learning Helping Skills

There is no enterprise more complex than helping someone work through a difficult problem. Often, the person cannot articulate clearly what is most bothersome. Professionals often do not agree on the most accurate diagnosis, much less the preferred treatment strategy. Even when people do appear to make progress in sessions, they are not necessarily making lasting changes in their lives. To complicate matters further, sometimes the people you think are cooperating the most with your efforts do not actually apply outside of sessions what they have supposedly learned. They may report that that things are getting better when, in fact, nothing much has changed. In other cases, you may feel frustrated that you do not appear to be doing much good at all when the person is really quite different, even though the reports sound discouraging.

Why Be a Helper?

Regardless of your chosen field, becoming a helper brings incredible satisfaction in knowing that you have made a difference in people's lives. The skills you learn to promote greater self-awareness and understanding, as well as to promote constructive action, work equally well in your own life as they do with those who approach you for assistance. You will find that the more you learn about helping others, the better you will become at enhancing all of your relationships.

Why do people seek professional help in the first place? The most obvious answer is because they cannot handle things on their own. They have already exhausted all the internal options that have been available, and they find that what may have worked in the past is no longer providing needed relief. In many cases, they are not seeking help out of personal choice, but rather because they are being forced to do so by family members, the court system, or others in positions of authority. It is not only normal that people will feel a certain ambivalence, if not outright resistance, to help that you offer, but also to be expected.

People may consult you for a variety of reasons—they feel depressed or anxious or out of control; they are having problems with family or friends; they are struggling with addictions; they are unhappy in school, their jobs, or at home; they feel trapped or lost or confused; they seek guidance about the future; they wish to understand the present; they want to live more in the present; they seek to overcome procrastination, inertia, underachievement, poor school, or job performance—the list is endless. Yet in most of these situations, and in the variety of problems and issues you will encounter, there are some fairly universal concepts and helping skills that will serve you well in your efforts to provide assistance. As an added bonus, most helping relationships can potentially change you for the better, just as they transform others.

Changes in the Field

Helping relationships have traditionally taken months, if not years, to promote significant relief of symptoms. Changes in the professional landscape precipitated by the managed care movement have led to briefer forms of intervention, as well as increased accountability by practitioners regarding what they believe is the problem, what they propose to do about it, and what specific, identifiable, results are observed.

The originators of counseling and therapy, theorists such as Sigmund Freud and Carl Rogers, would hardly recognize the current scene. Brief therapies are now the order of the day. Group and family structures are rapidly replacing individual sessions as the preferred choice. No longer can it be expected that any therapeutic approach will be applied universally without considering the gender and cultural background of each client. A new generation of medications is being used routinely for treating depression, panic disorders, and other emotional problems that previously were treated with counseling alone. These drugs are not only more effective than their predecessors, but they also have fewer side effects.

There have been dramatic changes in the past few years, not only in how helping is done, but also in how professionals are trained. New innovations in teaching methods, supervision strategies, and technology have made it possible to proceed in an orderly, logical path along the journey of helping others. Training methods are now far more integrative, often including components that involve content, skill development, supervised practice, experiential learning, field studies, simulations, online instruction, and internships.

What all this means is that the training that you will receive is quite different from what took place just a decade ago. Consider that in another decade what you are learning now may be just as obsolete. This is one reason why the helping professions are such a dynamic, exciting discipline to study. Although some concepts and approaches remain somewhat stable, other facets evolve in as little as a few years. This means that your commitment to becoming a helper will hardly end with your formal education; learning will involve a lifelong devotion.

A Daunting Journey

Taking into account the ambiguous, abstract nature of helping relationships; the severity of intractable, chronic problems; and the limited time and resources currently available to a make a difference, it is no wonder that professional helpers need years of training to do their jobs properly. Whether functioning as a social worker, psychologist, psychiatrist, counselor, teacher, family therapist, nurse, mental health specialist, minister, or human resource worker, several years are often invested to learn the basic approaches and put them into practice. This includes, but is not limited to, theories of human learning; physical, social, intellectual, moral, emotional, and spiritual growth; interpersonal behavior in families and groups; multicultural perspectives; educational and vocational development; ethical and legal issues; research and evidence-based methods; and the assortment of various intervention approaches. In addition to this conceptual foundation, professionals learn several dozen core helping skills and a few hundred basic interventions that can be applied to individual, group, and family settings.

Perhaps you can appreciate why it takes a long time, and such an investment of time and energy, to become highly skilled as a helper. Once theory is learned and skills are mastered, it takes years to accumulate enough experience with diverse clients to feel confident and reasonably effective.

It may, therefore, seem presumptuous to create a primer that purports to cover the essence of helping in such a modest volume. How on earth can you possibly learn all there is to know to help people? The answer, rather obviously, is that you cannot grasp all of it in a single dose, no matter how clearly, concisely, and accessibly the material is presented. The intent of this book is to get you started.

Making a Difference

It so happens that with some basic background, some introductory concepts, a few core skills, and some elegantly simple strategies, you can make a difference in people's lives in a reasonably short period of time. No longer must helping take years in the hands of doctors to work well. Recent studies have demonstrated that beginning helpers, teachers, paraprofessionals, even high-school-age peer counselors with as little as a few weeks training, can have a significant, positive effect on those they are helping. When goals are limited, specific skills are employed, interventions are targeted, and supervision is available, it is entirely feasible to promote lasting changes.

Although the goal of this book—to teach you helping skills—is somewhat ambitious, the scope of our mission will be rather modest. We will concentrate on the more basic concepts and skills that you will need to get started immediately in service to others. Because this is an accelerated training program of sorts, it is critical that you find ways to practice the ideas in your life and work. After all, you cannot learn helping (or anything else) from a book unless you put the concepts into action. Although there will be opportunities for you to experiment and practice with classmates, you will find helping skills to be just as useful in your personal life—with your friends, family, coworkers, and other loved ones. In fact, one of the most absolutely amazing aspects of this field is that everything you learn to make yourself a skilled helper also makes you a more compassionate, responsive human being. When you learn to listen carefully, assess systematically, analyze logically, respond empathically, confront nondefensively, and problem solve creatively, you are also able to apply these methods to areas of your own life. So if you are really serious about mastering the skills of helping, I urge you to look for as many opportunities as possible to use the methods on a daily basis.

Personal Qualities

Although this is a primer about helping skills, this enterprise is as much about *being* as it is *doing*. In other words, who you are is as important as how you behave. Effective helpers are well trained in the theory, research, and skills that underlie their craft, but they also convey certain personal qualities that make them most influential and competent. If you consider what characteristics you would want in a helper, some traits come to mind immediately:

- Kindness and caring
- Interpersonal sensitivity

- Self-confidence and poise
- Emotional stability
- Flexibility and openness
- Noncritical and nonjudgmental
- Wisdom
- Morals and ethics

There are other qualities that might be important to you as well, depending on your own values and preferences, but most of all, you would want a helper who can actually practice in his or her own life what he or she is teaching to you. You would want someone who is actually living the same principles that he or she espouses are important for others. This means that effective helpers are good at applying all their skills and knowledge to improve the quality of their own lives in every important dimension—physically, emotionally, intellectually, morally, and spiritually.

As you read the list of important qualities for a helper, you cannot help but take inventory of your own functioning in each of these areas. The good news that lies ahead is that no matter how limited you feel in any one area (sensitivity or wisdom or stability or flexibility), you will find yourself growing far more fully functioning as you learn the skills of helping others.

Take Some Advice

In a brief primer such as this, the main goal is to get you started with basic helping skills in a way that increases your confidence, sense of competence, and positive outcomes as quickly as possible. As a beginner, it is also important that you practice safely, ethically, and cautiously—even if you do not help someone the way you had hoped, at least you do not want to hurt them. Such negative results happen most often when you (a) push people to do things for which they are not ready or prepared, (b) are disrespectful or insensitive to people's unique values or needs, (c) impose your own values on others, (d) attempt to meet your own needs, or (e) tell people what to do with their lives so *you* can feel better.

I am now about to violate one of the major cautions for beginning helpers: Don't give advice! There are several reasons for this admonishment, some of them fairly obvious. For one, people do not usually listen to advice in the first place; if they did, helping would be a simple matter of telling people what to do with their lives. Even if you give in to this impulse, usually to make yourself feel less helpless in the presence of others' pain, it is rare that anyone will respond as you imagine: "Gee, I hadn't thought of that.

Thanks so much for straightening things out for me! If you don't mind, I'll just leave right now so I can immediately go out and do what you suggest."

I don't know about you, but people rarely do what I tell them to do anyway, even when I think I know best. Imagine an adolescent boy walks downstairs in the morning with a shirt in each hand, one red and one blue.

"Dad," he says in a sleepy, irritable, morning voice, "which one of these shirts should I wear with these pants?" He is holding out a pair of fairly ordinary jeans.

The parent knows this is a trick question, but he cannot see where the trap is. It seems obvious to him that the red shirt is the way to go. He takes a deep breath and offers his advice: "Well, they're both nice shirts, but I guess I prefer the red one. With those pants, I mean."

"The red one!" the boy spits out in disgust. "Why *that* one?" He then turns around and heads back to his room, only to reappear a few minutes later wearing the blue one.

This is not an unusual situation. We all think we know what is best for others: whether they should wear their hair short or long, get divorced or stay married, quit their job or stick it out, get an abortion or have the baby, buy a sports car or a hybrid vehicle, confront their boss or let things slide. The problem is that even if your advice is perfectly correct (and there is rarely a way to know that), if you tell people what to do, you are reinforcing the idea that they need someone like you to make their decisions in the future.

If, on the other hand, what you tell people to do turns out as a disaster, you are the one who will get blamed for the outcome. Most people do not want to be responsible for the choices they make in life, so they are delighted to have a scapegoat they can hold accountable if things do not go the way they prefer.

Finally, I don't know about you, but I rarely know what's best for me at any given moment. How am I supposed to know what is best for you or anyone else when I agonize over whether to order the salmon or swordfish on the menu? How can I know for certain which way you should go when I have so many doubts about the direction I am headed? Much of the time, whether as a pedestrian or a helper, I feel lost.

In spite of these warnings to the contrary, there are some instances when giving advice is warranted, especially when research and experience show consistently a predictable pattern that can be anticipated. It is for this reason that lawyers, nurses, doctors, and other helping professionals have few compunctions about telling you what is in your best interests.

Although the advice I am about to give you for the best ways to learn helping may not fit your situation and style, I think you will find most of these points useful. But don't take my word for it; ask others in the field what helped them the most. That, in fact, is the very first point.

Find Professionals Who Are Doing What You Want to Do

Identify individuals who are working in a setting that most appeals to you. Interview them. Ask them how they got to where they are now. What helped them the most? What helped them the least? What do they wish they had done differently?

One of the best ways to learn helping is to watch the best ones in action. One easy thing to do is to check out all the masters on tape or DVD. Your school library or department is likely to own demonstration videos in which the most prominent practitioners show how they work with clients, often in actual sessions.

There is no substitution, however, for seeing the real thing live. You may be fortunate enough to be able to arrange to sit in on a group session or perhaps to watch counseling from behind a one-way mirror.

Get Counseling for Yourself

If observing master helpers gives you a valuable perspective, actually experiencing the role of client may be even better. Many veterans believe that among all their training experiences, being a client helped them the most. You come to know, not just in your head but in your heart, what really works. You can sell your services more convincingly because you have seen the results, up close and personal. Finally, being a helper is not only about *doing* things, but also about *being* a particular way. The confidence, poise, serenity, and compassion that are so important in helping cannot be faked easily; you must become a more fully functioning human being.

Record Yourself and Solicit Feedback

One of the most enlightening aspects of training involves the critical examination of your helping behavior. Perhaps you are not aware that you raise your voice at the end of sentences, diminishing the power of your interventions by turning everything into a question. Maybe you have not realized how bored you appear at times. Also common in beginners is the overuse of interrogatory questions and a great need to fill any silence with "noise." These mistakes, plus any other patterns, will become obvious once you can review your performance and receive critical, yet supportive, feedback from experts. In fact, it may very well be part of your class that you will tape yourself while practicing helping skills and then receive feedback from your instructor.

Once you become introduced to a new skill—for example, the use of rephrasing as a means to promote deeper exploration—record a brief session with a friend or classmate in which you practice what you learned. Listen to the recording several times, critiquing your own behavior. It is even more useful to make a typescript of the conversation to review in greater detail. After you have analyzed the session, recruit the assistance of a more experienced helper to debrief you and make suggestions. This is, by far, one of the best ways to become a more critical observer of your own helping efforts. It is also exciting to hold on to these samples of your work so that you can note improvements over time.

Volunteer to Work With Someone You Admire

Colead a group with a more experienced helper. The crucial variable here is that your partner is truly an expert in ways that you would like to be; otherwise, you might develop bad habits from watching and working with someone who knows less than you do.

It might seem difficult to find opportunities in which you can actually practice helping, even under the direct supervision of a trained professional. You would be surprised, however, how many agencies and organizations are staffed by paraprofessionals who have mostly learned on the job. Many other experts trained at the graduate level may also be open to working with an apprentice.

Increase Your Tolerance for Ambiguity

Helping is one of those disciplines in which there are few right answers or clear solutions to problems. Often, people do not know what is really bothering them; if they do think they know, it might not be the real issue that needs to be addressed. To make matters worse, people are sometimes not honest with themselves, much less with you, so it is hard to determine what is true.

It is not unusual that some of those people who you believe you helped the most will not even acknowledge the progress, much less show gratitude for your efforts. To further confuse matters, there are some people you will try to help who do not seem to have changed a bit, even after many conversations, yet others will report dramatic progress outside of sessions. There are times you will find it difficult to figure out what the real issues are in someone's life; he or she may not be able to articulate what is at the core. Then when transformations do take place, you may never know what it is that you said or did that made the most difference.

The issues that people struggle with are often complex, abstract, and difficult to describe. What solution do you offer someone who wants to find meaning in her life? What concrete plan do you come up with for someone who doesn't so much want to change anything as he wants to understand himself better? What specific steps do you take with a client who wants to explore her relationship with God or who seeks to find some deeper purpose for the recent death of a loved one? What do you say to someone who cannot even tell you exactly what is most bothersome?

The answer to all these challenges is that you had better develop a great deal of patience and tolerance for the ambiguous, complex nature of human struggles. In many cases, there are no single, correct answers; sometimes, you cannot even figure out what the questions are. Although it is certainly helpful in some situations to proceed in an orderly, sequential, problem-solving style, in other cases, you will be exploring unknown territory without a compass or a map. You had better get used to feeling lost.

Solicit Recommendations of Important Books

Read them. Do not just restrict yourself to professional books, but also check out fiction and trade books that describe the nature of human change. Certain novels, biographies, and other genres provide a glimpse of how people cope with adversity (see the suggestions at the end of this and other chapters).

Ask your instructors, as well as professionals in the field, to recommend a list of books that they consider "must reading" for any literate helper. Do not let yourself feel overwhelmed: Hundreds of such suggestions will be made. Start with the few that are mentioned most frequently.

Immerse Yourself in Different Cultures

So much of helping involves the ability to enter the world of those you are trying to help. This means learning their unique cultures, family histories, languages, customs, values, and priorities. It means being able to transcend the "differentness" between you and others so that you can help from their perspective rather than imposing your values on them. This is especially the case with those clients who are not from the "majority culture," meaning white, Anglo-Saxon males. Of course, what constitutes minority status, especially an oppressed people, will vary from location to location.

You will most likely receive some training in multicultural or cross-cultural issues. Although this formal coursework is invaluable to familiarize you with the importance of adapting methods to fit the unique cultural context for each person, it may have its limits. Prejudices, biases, and racist beliefs are so deeply rooted they are not easily changed by intellectual challenges alone; often, something fairly dramatic is needed.

It is especially useful to identify some culture about which you do not have much experience and that would represent a significant proportion of your future clients. I am not referring here to only ethnicity, such as the case of African American, Vietnamese American, or Mexican American cultures. I am using the term *culture* broadly to include any group of people who share similar values and context for their experience. This could include cultures such as "feminists," "rural small town residents," "gays and lesbians," "construction workers," "Mormons," "West Texans," or "accountants." Culture can thus be determined by geography, religious affiliation, sexual orientation, and a variety of other factors that shape who people are and how they experience the world.

Travel as much as you can, and when you do, make an effort to learn the customs of each place you visit. Suspend your own orientation and preferences so that you can appreciate the unique perspectives of people who live in quite different ways than you are used to. Make an effort to control your tendency to judge others who live in ways you do not appreciate or understand.

Create Support Groups Among Peers

Learning the skills of helping is not only intellectually challenging but emotionally draining. You will likely experience a lot of stress along the way, not the least of which will result from performance anxiety about whether you are cut out for this type of work. There is no way that you can delve deeply into other people's pain without being profoundly affected in the process. Some experienced practitioners believe that despair is contagious; when you get close to people who are miserable, conflicted, or just downright ornery, you will be touched by their anguish. Your buttons will continually be pushed when you face the exact issues that you fear the most. Again and again, you may see yourself, including your own unresolved stuff, in every session you conduct.

It is for this reason that you will need lots of support from family and friends along the way. Sometimes, even that is not nearly enough. You might decide to seek professional help if stress symptoms become too disruptive. At the very least, you may wish to join (or begin) a support group of your peers so that you have a regular forum to work through the accumulated pressures you face. This group should not be a "bitch session" in which you take turns complaining and whining about how unfair the world is, how uncooperative your clients are, and how unappreciated and underpaid you feel. Neither should you use the time to problem solve and give advice (I hope I was convincing earlier about urging you to avoid this). Instead, you can use the group to hear one another and to offer encouragement and support. You will find immeasurable relief in just realizing you are not alone in your struggles.

Ask Lots of Questions

There is much you will be exposed to, in this book as well as in your coursework, that will not make a lot of sense. One of the common issues of beginners is the feeling that you are not good enough or that you are not as smart or talented as your peers. As such, there is reluctance to ask questions about things you do not understand, out of fear that this will give you away as the fraud you really believe yourself to be.

I can recall vividly, for example, being utterly confounded by the assortment of different helping approaches, all of which seemed to work effectively. Each instructor or supervisor had a different style, some in direct contradiction to others I had seen, yet they all seemed to be convinced that their method was right and others were wrong. I so badly wanted to ask how it was possible that you could help people effectively by reflecting their feelings, challenging their irrational beliefs, constructing an alternative narrative, or realigning the power hierarchies in their families, but I did not want to reveal how stupid I felt. It was only after I was out in the field for a while that I realized that few people really understand this as well as they think they do.

If you do not feel safe asking questions in class, then start cataloguing them in your notes or journal. Once you can secure some private time from patient supervisors, mentors, and experienced professionals, you can address your questions then. Be prepared, however, to hear some contradictory answers from two (or more) equally skilled professionals (remember the point earlier about increasing your tolerance for ambiguity and uncertainty).

Keep a Journal

Helping is, by its very nature, a reflective activity. You are continually called on to make sense of confusing situations, to decode underlying feelings, and to unravel mysteries that have previously gone overlooked. This analytic mindset does not come naturally for most; it is a learned way of looking at the world. One of the most useful vehicles for training yourself to think like a helper is to use a journal to record your impressions and experiences (see Table 1.1 for some examples).

Journaling is a time-honored method employed by writers who jot down ideas for stories, as well as character sketches that may find their way into published material at a later time. In the same sense, helpers need a safe repository to store plans for the future, not to mention a place to debrief themselves after a poignant or stressful session.

Table 1.1   What to Write in a Journal

Type of Entry	Example
Personal note	*I notice that I become defensive whenever the instructor calls on me. I want to read something about defensive mechanisms and what they mean.*
Dumping	*I am so sick of my parents intruding in my life. They won't respect my boundaries, no matter how many times I tell them I need my privacy.*
Introspection	*I wonder what it means that I have such a high need for people to like me. I go to such extreme lengths to win others' approval.*
Processing insight	*I seem to have trouble with confrontation. I think this is related to the ways I was punished when I was younger.*
Dialogue with instructor	*I really like it when you use personal examples from your life to illustrate the ideas in class. I wish, though, that you gave us more time to talk in groups.*
Goal setting	*I've got to get better organized with my studies and work schedule or I'm never going to catch up. I will spend one hour studying each night this week.*
Creative expression	*I feel lost. Wandering around. But lost is good. It means I can't be found. Except when I'm ready.*
Rehearsal	*When I see my brother, I'm going to tell him: "You can't keep expecting me to be there for you when . . ." No, I need to say it without complaining.*
Self-talk	*Every time I get myself in a situation like this, I back off. It's all about avoiding conflict. I need to try something different next time.*

Although journals may be useful to help you remember important ideas, categorize significant insights, work through difficult cases, play back confusing dialogue, and draw together important connections, they are also critical to help you metabolize things going on in your own life. Because helping requires a high degree of clarity and serenity on the part of its practitioners, you will need a way to work on your own problems that crop up along the way.

Practicing helping skills leaves you no place to hide from your own unresolved issues. The people you try to help will push your buttons (accidentally or on purpose to prevent you from getting too close). They will struggle with gut-wrenching themes that you can easily relate to—fear of losing control, fear of mediocrity, loneliness, growing old, abandonment, failure, intimacy, stagnation, enmeshment, or helplessness. Every conversation you undertake with a needy person is likely to stir up a whole host of problems that you thought were resolved long ago.

A journal becomes a place where you can write every week, or every day, recording the things you have learned, the insights you want to remember, the goals you have for the future, and the issues you need help with yourself. You can practice your helping skills on yourself, especially new techniques that have not yet been field tested. Finally, you can talk to yourself in an honest, authentic way, knowing that your written words will hold you accountable in the future.

Go to Conferences and Workshops

Academic pressures do inspire a degree of commitment that would be difficult without this structure. You are forced to read, study, and practice in ways that you would not do otherwise. Writing papers, taking exams, giving oral presentations, and doing other assignments require you to devote time and energy to your training. Nevertheless, there are limits to what can be done in the classroom. Besides, tests and grades often get in the way of learning, because you may be as concerned with how your performance is being evaluated as you are with actually learning the material.

As a way to supplement your schoolwork, you would be well advised to attend as many conferences and workshops as you can afford. Besides the networking opportunities that are available to meet and interact with other professionals, there is a very different atmosphere in workshops than in the classroom. There tends to be a greater focus on practical applications and cutting-edge innovations that is often not possible in school, given the priority on providing background concepts. Second, you can pick and choose the workshops that fit your interests and specialties.

If workshops supply intensive study and practice during concentrated periods, then conferences provide a smorgasbord of offerings in a longer time frame. You can attend a half-dozen different sessions per day, if that is your priority. Others may prefer the informal interactions that take place during social encounters. You can make new friends, generate job opportunities, exchange ideas, and find support among hundreds of others who do the same thing that you do.

Involve Your Friends and Family, or They Will Be Left Behind

One of the exciting, yet disconcerting, phenomena often observed by newcomers to the field is the number of ways that you will change as a result of your training. Just as you will become more sensitive and interpersonally skilled, so too will your standards for intimate relationships change and grow. You may find yourself hungering for more intense engagement with others because you will have had a taste of such encounters with your clients. You may grow intolerant and impatient with superficial conversations. You will notice things about your family and friends that have previously been beyond your awareness. In short, you will become transformed into a different person altogether—someone who is more powerful, influential, and persuasive, yet also more empathic and compassionate.

Although you may be delighted with these changes in your personality, others may not be so impressed. In fact, some of your friends and family members may be threatened by what you have become. They may not like the ways you are more direct and assertive. They may resent the steps you are taking to improve yourself. Worst of all, they may fear being left behind.

Such worries of abandonment are neither unusual nor unrealistic. When one person makes a concerted effort to improve life skills, while others sit around doing the same old things, there may very well develop some distance between them. This is especially likely if you do not keep loved ones up to date on what you are learning.

You may very well decide to change some relationships after becoming aware of ways they have been unsatisfying or dysfunctional. Other relationships, however, can actually be improved if you apply the things you learn to your personal life. Let loved ones know how much you appreciate them. Make an effort to initiate more intimate conversations. Practice the listening and responding skills you learn. Finally, be patient with others as they struggle to adjust to the new you that is emerging.

Apply Everything You Learn to Your Own Life

Helping others is one of the few professions where it is not only possible, but highly desirable, to apply the theories and concepts to your own life. All of the things you will learn in class or in this text are not only useful for understanding people you want to help, but also yourself. All the strategies you will practice to motivate clients can work equally well with yourself. Each of the theories you will study can be personalized in such a way that you can supply examples from your own life to support the arguments made.

In the next chapter, it may seem at times that the various theories presented are unnecessarily complicated and esoteric. Trust me when I tell you that each of these models has something to offer, not only in your work helping others but also in understanding yourself better. In fact, before you can ever hope to translate the skills of helping into a natural style that fits your unique personality, you must first be able to apply what you know to yourself. Only then can you be a passionate and convincing advocate for the principles that you claim matter most.

For Review

- Change is difficult to measure and even harder to assess over time.
- Helpers are called on to be accountable for what they do, justifying their best practices and documenting their efforts.
- Many changes in helping have evolved in the last few years, making the process more responsive to cultural and gender differences.
- Mastering the skills of helping takes considerable time, commitment, training, and supervision, but a working knowledge can be achieved in a semester if you dedicate yourself to that mission.
- Helping is not synonymous with giving advice, a strategy that has many negative side effects.
- Taking a proactive stance toward your own learning is required to become a skilled and compassionate helper. The helping attitudes, skills, and strategies are internalized only through considerable reflection, practice, and feedback.

For Reflection and Practice

1. Start a journal, beginning right this moment, in which you write down your feelings, thoughts, reactions, fears, struggles, and goals related to anything that was triggered by this chapter or your class thus far.

2. Identify several helpers who are working in the sort of job that you would like some day. Interview them with respect to how they learned to become comfortable and effective in their helping skills. Ask their advice about what you can do to promote your own growth and development.

3. Think about a time in your life in which you were struggling terribly. What made the greatest difference to you in regaining your stability? Talk to someone (or classmates) you trust about who has been most helpful to you in your life and what that person did that was most influential and effective.

4. Write a plan describing the kind of helper you would like to be some day. Set specific goals for yourself, as well as a program for how you intend to reach your objectives.

5. Become aware of instances all around you in which people attempt to be helpful to others—teachers explaining ideas, parents disciplining their kids, someone giving directions. Note what a helper does specifically that appears to be most and least effective.

6. Ask trusted friends, family, and classmates for feedback on your personal attributes that might be most and least useful in your helping efforts.

7. Go to the library or bookstore and dip into several other books about the process of helping. Familiarize yourself with some of the journals in the field and look through several issues.

8. Go to the counseling center, a local agency, or a private practitioner and experience helping as a client. If you cannot think of anything else to work on, you can always sort through your uncertainty about the future, a conflicted relationship, or some lifelong theme that crops up again and again.

For Further Reading

Corey, M. S., & Corey, G. (2006). *Becoming a helper* (5th ed.). Pacific Grove, CA: Wadsworth.

Glicken, M. (2006). *Learning from resilient people: Lessons we can apply to counseling and psychotherapy.* Thousand Oaks, CA: Sage.

Kottler, J. A. (2003). *On being a therapist* (3rd ed.). San Francisco: Jossey-Bass.

Meier, S., & Davis, S. (2008). *Elements of counseling* (6th ed.). Belmont, CA: Wadsworth.

Pipher, M. (2005). *Letters to a young therapist.* New York: Basic Books.

Ram Das & Gorman, P. (1985). *How can I help? Stories and reflections on service.* New York: Knopf.

Rosenthal, H. (2004). *Before you see your first client.* New York: Routledge.

Yalom, I. (2003). *The gift of therapy.* New York: Perennial.

Some Novels That You Might Find Interesting

Mark Haddon, *The Curious Incident of the Dog in the Night-Time*

Jonathan Kellerman, *When the Bough Breaks*

Barbara Kingsolver, *The Poisonwood Bible*

Wally Lamb, *I Know This Much Is True*

Irvin Yalom, *Schopenhauer's Cure*

2

Theories of Helping

A ll the principles of this book are based on evidence derived from empirical research, theoretical conceptions, and clinical experience. In a brief primer, there is hardly space to cover the full gamut of theories available or to provide much detail about those that are included, but this overview will at least introduce you to some of the major forces that have led to the helping skills currently in practice.

In addition to the limitations of space, there are also considerations with respect to the biases of the traditional approaches that have had the greatest impact on helpers. Some of the biggest names in the field, such as Sigmund Freud (psychoanalysis), Carl Rogers (person-centered therapy), Albert Ellis (rational emotive therapy), Aaron Beck (cognitive behavior therapy), Fritz Perls (gestalt therapy), Alfred Adler (individual psychology), and William Glasser (reality therapy), were all older, white men who led relatively privileged lives. That does not mean that their theories were not useful for wide populations—just that they were limited in their applications in that they originally failed to account for huge ranges of diversity, especially with members of oppressed, marginalized, and minority groups (based on race, age, gender, culture, socioeconomic class, sexual orientation, physical challenges, and so on).

Since the time of their original development, all of these theories have been further refined, researched, and evolved to make them more responsive to the needs of a multicultural society. Even more significant, a number of more contemporary helping approaches have been developed specifically for this purpose.

Internalizing Theories

"I was driving down the highway one afternoon," a student relates with emotion in his voice, "when I saw this car crash right in front of me. It was terrible. There was wreckage everywhere and I could hear people moaning and crying."

The student pauses for a moment to regain his composure. Tears are pooling in his eyes. He takes a deep breath and continues.

"I didn't even think about what I was doing. I just jumped out of my car and ran to the scene, hoping I could do something to help. I saw this little boy sitting alone on a hill. He looked battered but seemed to be okay physically. At least nothing to be broken. But he looked devastated and very worried: It was clear that his parents hadn't fared so well. In fact, I was pretty sure that one or both of them were dead."

The student looked at me helplessly. It was obviously difficult for him to talk about this, so I encouraged him as best I could.

"I just started to panic as I sat there with this kid. I tried to remember which theory I should use in a situation like this. I had just learned about crisis intervention but I couldn't remember a thing: I was blank.

"When the little boy started talking to me, asking for reassurance that his parents were okay, I knew that I had to do something. I just put all the theory stuff aside and held him. I tried to listen as best I could. I tried to be with him with all of me. I forget which theory that was, but frankly, there was just no time to sort it all out."

Naturally, this student was following a theory that guided what he should do, even if he could not articulate it at the time. You will know that you have really understood a theory when you don't have to think about it, when it has become part of you.

What Theories Can Do for You

Perhaps it is not necessary to convince you that a study of conceptual frameworks will make your life easier. After all, you have favorite theories of your own that you use every day. You predict what the driver ahead of you will do next based on a thorough study of his tendencies during the preceding minutes that you have been stuck in traffic behind him. You have a theory to explain where you are in life, as well as one to account for what has held you back. You have theories that guide your eating and other lifestyle choices. Any time you are confronted with something you don't understand, you construct a theory to make sense of the phenomenon. With respect to helping situations, theories are invaluable for a number of reasons that may not be readily apparent.

Organize Information

The challenge of most helping situations is not a scarcity of data but having too much information. What pieces of the puzzle are most relevant? Which ones fill in the important image versus those that just take up space, or worse yet, belong to other puzzles? Which pieces are missing?

In any initial interview, usually lasting somewhere from 30 to 90 minutes, you can collect an extraordinary amount of information from a client. When you add to the pile the various questionnaires and intake forms that are usually completed, plus any assessment instruments that were administered, it could take years to organize all the data, much less make sense of them.

What you need is a theoretical framework that tells you how to sort and organize the information you have collected. You have background on the presenting symptoms and when they first began. You know about the person's family history as well as current living situation. You have access to medical records. You have a complete battery of tests that were administered that tell you about the person's coping style, defense mechanisms, personality features, deceptive tendencies, perceptual distortions, intellectual functioning, and problem-solving skills. During your first interview, you learned about educational background, career plans, and social life. During your observations of this individual, you could write a book about all the mannerisms you observed, the interesting ways that the person expresses himself or herself.

Now, the question is, What do you do with all this stuff?

What you need is an organizing framework that tells you what information is most important, what aspects to attend to first, and which can be set aside, at least temporarily. Ideally, such a model will help you create some sort of meaning from the data available, often in partnership with the client as a consultant. You would also find it useful if you could formulate a working diagnosis, as well as several suggested courses of action that could be tried.

Provide a Framework for Action

Before you can do something, you've first got to have a plan for what you want to accomplish. Do you want to work on trust issues in the relationship first? Do you want to solicit the cooperation of other family members to join in on the sessions? Perhaps it would be best to explore previous attempts to solve the problem, or maybe look for exceptions in which the person has felt successful keeping the problem at bay.

You can't just pick a strategy by the seat of your pants. It may seem as if experienced practitioners are operating by whim or gut instinct, but they are really just taking shortcuts based on an abbreviated theory that they have been employing for years. You would hardly want a surgeon to operate on you because she sensed it would be good for you. You would hardly approve a mechanic to undertake expensive repairs on your car because it felt like the right thing to do. You would want to know the reasoning behind the recommendation. Your clients will feel much the same way.

One good guideline is not to attempt any intervention unless you have a defensible rationale that you can articulate. This may slow you down a bit, but this is not altogether a bad thing. Another good rule to follow is that even if you don't help anyone, you do not want to hurt them. Such caution will make you carefully assess exactly what you are trying to accomplish and how your choice of intervention follows the theory you follow.

For example, I notice as I see you reading the last paragraph that you have a puzzled look on your face. I want to say something to put you at ease, but before I do, I want to make sure that I am reading you correctly. Perhaps you are not confused at all, but merely concentrating, or maybe what looks like befuddlement to me might really be anger or resentment, or even boredom.

I've decided that because I don't yet know you very well, I can't be certain what is going on. My intervention must, therefore, be tentative and cautious. Hopefully, I can even come up with something that could be interpreted in many different ways so that you will feel understood by me no matter which way you interpret my response.

My theory-in-action is that trust between us will be built on my ability to read accurately what you are feeling and thinking. Furthermore, helping you work through initial hesitance will lead to a closer alliance between us that will prove useful later when we move into areas that might be more threatening. Based on this framework, I want to be careful not to frighten you or push you away. I will thus choose a reasonably safe intervention at this point, perhaps a neutral encouraging lead like, "I notice that you are looking thoughtful after reading that last passage."

Even if you were, in fact, bored or not thinking at all about what you read, I've still conveyed my intense interest in how you are doing so far. As we come to know each other better, my responses would hit the mark more and more often. This is how my theory becomes more useful over time, constantly making adjustments in light of new experience.

Impress People

Seriously, this is important. Much of your influence over others comes from their perception that you know lots of good stuff that they want.

Unless people perceive you as a knowledgeable expert and someone who is highly skilled, they are unlikely to listen to what you have to say.

On many occasions, a client's greatest fear stems from not understanding what is happening to him or her. You will be asked to provide some sort of explanation, a theory of sorts, to account for what happened and why.

Imagine, for example, that someone is quite disturbed over a recent pattern in which she continues to pick untrustworthy friends in whom to confide her most cherished secrets. Each time, she has been betrayed, or at least, that is the way it seems to her. This woman considers herself an excellent judge of character and not previously prone to self-destructive behavior, so she is extremely puzzled about what all this means. Is she looking for trouble? Is this part of some previously undiagnosed interpersonal problem? Perhaps she isn't betrayed at all, you suggest to her very carefully.

"Whatever do you mean?" she asks indignantly, signaling that you are moving too fast with her, confronting her about something she isn't yet ready to examine.

"I don't mean to imply this is your fault," you quickly interject, not at all sure that this isn't *exactly* what you meant. You are operating from a theory that looks at most interpersonal behavior as a form of reciprocal influence. You recognize that your client would prefer to place blame on her friends; that way, she isn't responsible for her own misery. You believe that what seems to her like betrayal is probably behavior on the part of others that doesn't meet her preferred expectations.

When you explain this theory to your client, her response is cautious and curious: "So, what you're saying is that these people aren't doing this to me, but rather I'm somehow setting myself up for disappointment."

You nod enthusiastically. You are proud of how quickly she is picking up on this theory.

"Well," she says with an exasperated sigh, "I can't say that I'm pleased hearing this. I quite liked thinking it was all my friends' fault for letting me down."

This two-minute interaction, although dramatic in its brevity, is not unusual during effective helping. There are times when moments of opportunity will arise, perfect instances to introduce a theory to explain what might be going on.

Of course, just as often, your theory will miss the mark or not be well received. That's fine, though: There are plenty of other theories you can try later.

Create Illusions of Truth

There are those who believe that theories are not designed to help clients but to ease the minds of helpers. Without theories that give us some landmarks for our work, we would feel even more lost. Our theories might not truly reflect truth or reality, any more than a map can be completely accurate and contain all needed information, but they represent working models that get us where we want to go most of the time.

Treat theories not as the last word on the way things are, but as the best guides currently available. Read research critically to check out how well certain theories translate into effective action. Better yet, conduct your own research by testing theories in your own work setting with your unique client population.

Theories You Should Know About

It would probably take at least 2 to 3 years of full-time study to become reasonably proficient in the various theories that helpers use routinely (that is why people get advanced degrees and spend a lifetime trying to master the field). That is not to say that as a beginner, you cannot get a running start after a brief perusal of the basic concepts. For now, do not worry about the names of those who invented the theories, nor should you be concerned about learning all the specific terms favored by each model. There will be plenty of time for that in future courses.

At this point, there are a few basic concepts that you should grasp. As a helper, you will want to have at your fingertips some sort of models to understand (a) how people learn, (b) how they develop in each of several realms of experience, (c) how they develop problems, and (d) what can be done to restore some sort of stable footing.

Some final words of caution: Keep in mind that there are three or four whole courses devoted to the material contained in this chapter alone. I hesitated even including mention of these theories in a primer book such as this, because the emphasis is on practical application. I am at a loss, however, as to how to introduce you to the helper's skills and strategies without at least giving you the most rudimentary background in their theoretical grounding. The intention here is not to burden you with a bewildering array of names and confusing terms but rather to impress you with some of the background ideas that developed the most effective techniques. Because a little book such as this can present only a brief overview of the theories, you will want to peruse some of the resources in the "For Further Reading" section for additional information.

Developmental Theories

There are more theories than you can imagine to explain how people grow and develop. Whereas, at one time, human development was treated as a linear progression through successive stages (most of the action taking place during the first decade of life), contemporary thinking now recognizes that personalities and behavioral patterns do not stabilize until well into adulthood. Furthermore, because of the enormous amount of change we face each year, adult development is more cyclical than linear in its evolution.

Nevertheless, from a historical perspective, theories of development were typically organized around various facets of human experience. Summarized in the following are several of the most prominent theories (unfortunately, this list is by no means exhaustive):

- *Physical development.* The developmental tasks that are appropriate for each age and stage in life, such as crawling, walking, and using language.
- *Emotional development.* The appropriate forms of emotional sensitivity and expression that are typically required in the culture.
- *Cognitive development.* The intellectual feats that are required for effective functioning, such as learning to think abstractly.
- *Psychosocial development.* The social behaviors that are needed to get needs met.
- *Moral development.* The stage of moral reasoning that allows people to make decisions and live with the consequences.
- *Family development.* The typical state of functioning that is associated with particular stages, from early courtship to the launching of a first child.
- *Spiritual development.* The convictions that guide core beliefs.
- *Cultural identity development.* The worldview that is often associated with members of particular groups.
- *Gender and sexual development.* The dominant identity associated with sex roles and sexuality.

Before you protest that you can never expect to learn all this in a single lifetime, consider that much of this you already know based on your own life experience.

In spite of the different emphases favored by each theory, most of them follow several premises:

1. *Development typically proceeds in a relatively orderly sequence.* This means that if you know what stage someone is currently functioning at, then you can predict where he or she is headed next, with a little friendly persuasion from you along the way.

2. *People progress naturally from one stage to another.* Normative data exist that help you understand where people are in relation to others who hold similar characteristics. Keep in mind, however, that individual differences often make people in groups vary more than those between groups. Also remember that some individuals may cycle back through previous stages as they encounter new life challenges.

3. *People do not generally skip stages.* You do not go from crawling to running, from babbling to speaking in metaphors, or from a completely enmeshed family to one in which every member functions independently.

There are many other conclusions that can be drawn from the literature on human growth and development. The main ideas may be adapted in such a way that you can assess how people are behaving in their lives compared with where they might be expected to be. Furthermore, once you know where and how people are functioning in various developmental arenas, you can make some informed choices about how to encourage their growth to the next levels.

Learning Theories

It is critical to understand not only how people grow naturally, but also how they learn. After all, helping is really about teaching people to unlearn dysfunctional patterns and substitute other options that are more effective. To construct such a treatment plan, you must have some idea about the ways that people learn.

Although there are about a dozen major theories to explain changes in behavior, they all subscribe to the idea that learning involves a permanent behavioral change as a result of experience. This is contrasted with other behavior changes that result from maturation or growth (described in the previous section).

You already know more than you think about these theories, because many of their concepts have slipped into normal language usage. The notion, for example, that behavior is reinforced by factors in the environment is a direct result of behavioral theory. Another example of a learning theory application that you practice regularly is rehearsal—the repetition of a behavior until it becomes automatic. This is part of another theory called cognitive information processing.

If you ever hope to help people in a consistent, effective way, you will obviously need to understand how they learn and change, not to mention the best practices currently available to encourage such enhanced performance. At some future time, you will most likely be exposed to theories that are already familiar to you, like behaviorism, but also other approaches that may stimulate creative approaches to the subject. Some of the most common learning theories currently employed by helpers include the following:

- *Operant conditioning.* The systematic application of reinforcement principles to increase or decrease the likelihood of certain behaviors. When someone reports he or she has made progress, you smile and offer warm encouragement.

When someone else creates some disruption, you extinguish that behavior through some form of punishment.

- *Classical conditioning.* The presentation of a stimulus that elicits certain responses. If reinforcement theory presents a stimulus to reward or extinguish a particular response, then classical conditioning elicits a response from a stimulus. For example, a teacher clears his throat, signaling to the students that he is about to ask a difficult question.
- *Modeling.* People tend to imitate behaviors or attributes that they find desirable in others. You demonstrate ways to be firm and assertive when faced with difficult situations.
- *Cognitive information processing.* Sensory input enters short-term memory, then is encoded for long-term storage and retrieval. A person is taught cues for responding to various situations at work that previously have been misinterpreted.
- *Brain-based learning.* The brain processes experience through all the senses, searching for meaningful organization and patterns. A person finds it much easier to master a new idea when there is opportunity to involve all the senses, as well as the intellect, emotions, and behavior.
- *Constructivism.* The creation of meaning in a particular context of the person's life. A person with poor self-esteem and low confidence is helped to construct an alternative view of his or her life and situation.

This is a mere sampling of the theories currently in use. Again, I wish to reassure you that at this juncture, you should not be concerned with discriminating between the various models (a higher form of learning beyond appropriate levels for first exposure), but rather you should just understand that research has suggested a number of learning principles that you would be wise to follow in your work. A few of these guidelines include the following:

1. Learning stems from motivation. Make sure that the people you are helping are feeling stimulated to invest the hard work and energy involved in making changes.

2. Identify reinforcers for each individual that are likely to increase the frequency of effective behaviors and reduce maladaptive behavior.

3. Help people to practice new behaviors in a safe environment, because learning is inhibited by fear and stress.

4. Spend time exploring the cultural context for a person's behavior to understand its particular meaning.

5. Model the kinds of behavior that you would like to see others develop.

6. Involve as many of the senses as possible when teaching new information or concepts.

7. Help people connect what is being learned to their previous experience.

8. Deal with both conscious and unconscious processes.

9. Establish the kind of relationship that is most conducive to exploration, experimentation, and risk taking.

10. Make all helping attempts an active process in which the learner is fully and completely engaged as a partner in the outcome.

Theories of Intervention

It was a matter of personal preference to subdivide the various theories into those that specialize in explaining how learning occurs (previous section), those that concentrate more specifically on how people make personal changes in behavior (current section), and the ones that present models of intervention (next section). In practice, all three of these are interrelated. For example, there is a behavioral theory of learning, a behavioral theory of change, and a behavior therapy regimen. The same is true with regard to other approaches as well.

It is not particularly important for you to differentiate whether you need a theory of learning or intervention to help a given client. It is useful, however, to start generally and then move to the more specific.

This next group of theories represents the direct practical applications of those previously reviewed. Rather than concentrating on explaining behavior, however, this next batch is concerned primarily with moving people from one place to another. Each theory has its own distinct language and customs, just like foreign cultures. Naturally, this makes intercommunication between professionals difficult because each group speaks its own dialect.

Generally, a whole course is devoted to study of these next theories, so do not worry about getting them all straight. For now, try to familiarize yourself with their basic concepts, what strikes you about what they might have in common, or how they may appear most different. Generally, beginners are advised to follow one particular model that is most suitable for the setting and the clients with whom you will be working. It may seem obvious that you would use a different approach with substance-abusing teenagers than you would with corporate executives who wish to increase their productivity.

For the purposes of this book, a generic theory of intervention is employed that combines the best features of all the approaches. In practice, the vast majority of helpers describe themselves as "eclectic," meaning that they borrow favorite features of many theories. Depending on what someone needs at a particular moment and what kinds of problems are presented, you might employ a variety of intervention theories.

Psychoanalytic Theory

This approach, first ▓▓▓▓▓▓▓▓▓▓ has considerable historical value in contemp▓▓▓▓▓▓▓▓▓▓e still helpers who
favor this original app▓▓▓▓▓▓▓▓▓ted the methods to
contemporary practice. Some of the basic co▓▓▓ this theory include
the following:

- *The importance of the unconscious.* People are guided by motivations beyond their awareness.
- *Defense mechanisms.* People tend to ward off perceived threats with character-istic defenses, many of which you have probably heard of (rationalization, pro-jection, denial) because these terms have become part of normal language.
- *Transference.* Distortions will arise in the helping relationship that can be worked through as a means to address unresolved conflicts.
- *Countertransference.* Helpers, as well as their clients, may also distort what is going on in the relationship, sometimes having extreme reactions that are trig-gered by unresolved personal issues.
- *Catharsis.* People find some degree of relief if they are helped to tell their story and release negative feelings.

Contemporary practitioners, or those who are psychodynamically inclined, tend to value the importance of insight in their work, especially helping people to examine the ways their current struggles are reenactments of unresolved issues from the past. Whereas once this process represented a major long-term commitment of time, applications are now designed to work in a matter of months rather than years.

Client-Centered Theory

Carl Rogers and other humanists (those theorists who emphasize the helping relationship and stimulate the natural inclination toward growth) developed a theory based on the power of nurturing relationships that offer respect, acceptance, caring, and warmth. It was believed, most likely erro-neously, that these conditions were sufficient for change to take place. Although this may sometimes occur, there is often much more help needed to move people toward constructive action.

This theory believes helping should best take place by focusing on unex-pressed feelings, clarifying what a person experiences, and helping him or her to feel understood. The goal is to create greater self-awareness and self-responsibility, as well as to help people become more congruent and authen-tic. Remnants of this theory will be found in some of the basic skills you will soon be learning, especially those that involve reflecting underlying feelings.

Rogers and his proponents believed that most helping efforts, whether in education, counseling, or any human service, take place in a relationship that is trusting and respectful. Emphasis is placed on the *process* of learning, as well as the outcome. This means that considerable attention is not only directed toward what people are talking about and whether goals are reached, but also how people feel and perceive the experience.

Existential Theory

Similar to the approaches just mentioned, this theory advocates promoting insight and awareness, but it focuses on helping people create meaning in their lives. It represents an integration of a number of philosophers (Kierkegaard, Nietzsche), novelists (Dostoevsky, Turgenev), and helping professionals (Frankl, May, Yalom). Issues related to freedom, individual responsibility, alienation, and death are addressed, challenging people to explore who they are and where they are headed at their deepest levels.

This approach seems especially well-suited for individuals who have the time, ability, and inclination to explore the lack of meaning in their lives. Yet much of this theory has been integrated into other approaches that value the power of self-reflection to address life's most pressing questions related to human existence. Even in circumstances in which pain cannot be banished (chronic disease, trauma, Holocaust survivors), people can still be helped to find meaning in their suffering.

Gestalt Theory

Invented by another humanist, Fritz Perls, this existential theory has more direct practical application. It combines features from some of the theories mentioned earlier, especially with regard to dealing with unfinished business, but stresses more active strategies for helping people become more integrated and high functioning. Role playing is a common strategy employed, in which the client acts out scenarios in an attempt to come to terms with a conflict. Quite a number of other practical helping strategies were developed from this approach, many of which have now become standard operating procedure for any practitioner.

The focus of helping efforts is centered on the present, that is, how people are experiencing their bodies, internal reactions, and perceptions of others, right now in this moment. Increasing awareness of self and others is an important goal.

Individual Psychology

Alfred Adler, once a disciple of Freud's, went his own way to develop a theory that emphasizes much more about social context of behavior and the role of choice in making personal decisions. This theory is especially concerned with addressing a person's underlying feelings of inferiority, as well as the internal motivation to pursue social interests. As such, the helper explores mistaken or distorted thinking, encouraging people to develop a healthy lifestyle that is both satisfying and socially useful.

Many of Adler's original ideas can be found in cognitive, existential, and other therapies. He was among the first to encourage helpers to look at family or origin issues, to examine birth order and its effect on development, and to advocate that helpers take a stand for social justice issues.

Behavioral Theory

Covered earlier, this theory encourages helpers to be systematic in their interventions, devising methods that change specific, observable, and measurable behavior. Applying this model, you would help people declare specific goals, develop a plan to reach those goals, and then devise rewards for completing the therapeutic tasks. There is an important focus on identifying desired outcomes and then evaluating the extent to which these objectives have been met.

Behavioral approaches place a strong emphasis on developing homework assignments that help people practice new behaviors and generalize results to other areas of their lives. This approach is especially well-suited for specific behavioral problems such as addictions, bed-wetting, stuttering, bullying, as well as preventing stress.

Cognitive-Behavior Theory

Albert Ellis, Aaron Beck, and others created a theory that examines the ways that irrational thinking patterns and faulty logic lead people toward emotional suffering. If you change the way you think about things, alter your interpretation of reality, then you can alter the way you feel about it. This strategy of challenging a person's underlying assumptions has also become common practice among helpers, regardless of which theory they believe is most useful.

This is among the most commonly practiced theory for a wide variety of complaints because of its emphasis on teaching people new ways of looking at things in a relatively brief period of time. People are challenged to examine the ways they exaggerate disappointments, distort reality, make absolute demands of themselves or others that are unrealistic, and otherwise draw unreasonable conclusions based on limited data.

Reality Theory

William Glasser developed another action-oriented, problem-solving approach in which the helper works to maximize success experiences. Called "choice theory," people are urged to look at the consequences of their behavior, making changes according to their desired reality. This theory has been especially well adapted to work with addictions and in school settings.

Essentially, people are asked to consider two questions: (a) What is it that you are doing? and (b) How is what you are doing getting you what you want? People are thus helped to make responsible choices and then to accept responsibility for those decisions. If their stated needs are not being met by their current behavior, it is time to make different choices that will produce alternative outcomes.

Structural and Systemic Theory

These approaches stem from the family therapy movement and look at the ways individual behavior is the result of larger organizational systems. In contrast to the other models presented, which address primarily individual behavior, this theory looks at "circular causality"—the ways that one person becomes both the cause and effect of others' behavior. To change someone's behavior, you would need to work within the whole family or cultural system to which the person belongs.

The application of this theory involves exploring (a) patterns of interaction between a person and significant others, (b) ways the system is organized, (c) coalitions and alliances that exist between members of the system, and (d) power distribution in the system. This popular approach seeks to realign the balance in a family so that its members may function in more healthy ways.

Solution-Focused and Problem-Solving Theory

This is not so much a theory as an approach to helping that seeks relatively brief solutions to presenting problems without delving too much into the hows and whys. Proponents of this approach attempt to change behavior by disrupting the current dysfunctional system, forcing people to experiment with alternative actions. Symptoms are seen as a person's dysfunctional attempt to solve problems. Systematic attempts are made to experiment with strategies that are more likely to prove useful.

In this era of managed care, these approaches are becoming increasingly popular because of their brief interventions. Practitioners are encouraged to help people figure out what they are already doing that is not working and then to get them to experiment with alternatives.

Narrative Theory

This application of constructivist theory (mentioned in the previous section) seeks to help people create alternative stories about their lives. Problems are "externalized," meaning that people are taught to separate their symptoms from who they are. This theory is especially sensitive to the ways that people are indoctrinated into particular belief systems without allowing for individual, cultural, and gender differences.

Narrative therapy is based on the premise that people can be helped to rename and re-story their lives in far more empowering ways. The therapist acts as a collaborator rather than an expert, helping create narratives that lead to different perceived outcomes.

Feminist Theory

This theory arose in response to more conventional approaches that failed to recognize and respond to issues of culture, race, class, gender, and sexual orientation as they influence human experience. For the sake of convenience, included in this group might be other theories that are labeled as "relational" or "multicultural." They have in common a strong belief in advocacy and social justice, and in the examination of issues of power, control, and marginalization as they affect people and their relationships. Personal problems are thus viewed from a political and sociocultural lens that looks at the context in which difficulties emerged. A major goal is to increase a person's sense of empowerment.

Synthesis and Integration Models

There has been considerable convergence and integration of theories during the past few decades. A number of writers have been laboring to pull together the salient ingredients of most conceptual frameworks into a perspective that guides helping interventions. The boundaries between many

Table 2.1   Summary of Major Theories

Theory	Theorists	Assumptions	Skills
Psychoanalytic	Freud, Jung	Past influences present, unconscious motives influence behavior, defense mechanisms protect people against perceived threats	Interpretation, transference, dream analysis, working through resistance
Client-centered	Rogers	Focus on present, increasing awareness and expression of feelings, actualizing potential through a trusting relationship	Reflecting feelings, being fully present, practicing authenticity
Existential	Yalom, May	Explore meaning of life, issues of freedom, dread, fear of death, and responsibility; emphasis on living in the present	Confronting avoidance of responsibility, exploring issues of personal meaning
Gestalt	Perls	Seek to become more whole and integrated; emphasis on experience and increased awareness, living in the here and now	Confrontation, role playing, experimentation, group work
Individual	Adler	People motivated by feelings of inferiority as well as social interest; examining lifestyle and family issues	Lifestyle assessment, exploring early recollections
Behavioral	Krumboltz	Maladaptive behavior is reinforced and the product of learning; focus on specific goals and changing targeted behaviors	Modeling appropriate behavior, goal setting, rehearsal, homework
Cognitive	Beck, Ellis	Negative thoughts and irrational belief responsible for undesirable reactions and feelings	Disputing irrational thoughts and illogical beliefs
Reality	Glasser	People make choices that result in particular consequences	Exploring needs, wants, and choices; creating plans; moving toward action

Theory	Theorists	Assumptions	Skills
Systemic	Minuchin	Individual problems and solutions take place in a larger family system; behavior is viewed in an interactive context	Identifying coalitions and patterns, realigning hierarchies
Strategic	Haley, de Shazer, O'Hanlon	People develop problems because they are stuck doing the same maladaptive things over and over; focus on developing creative solutions	Reframing problems, using paradoxical directives, using hypnosis
Narrative	Neimeyer, White	There is no objective truth but rather there are multiple realities based on perceptions and experience; seek to help people to "re-story" their lives	Externalizing, curious questioning
Feminist	Jordan	Examine issues of power and control in the ways they limit possibilities; emphasize gender and cultural contexts	Facilitating empowerment collaborative, egalitarian relationships

theories have thus become blurred, just as their techniques and skills have become integrated into mainstream practice by almost everyone. It is not necessary to be a card-carrying cognitive therapist to dispute someone's irrational beliefs, just as it is no longer required to undergo years of training as a psychoanalyst to use dream analysis, interpretation, or transference work.

The majority of helpers now describe themselves as "eclectic" or "integrative," which means they borrow from a variety of approaches depending on

1. The presenting complaint
2. Cultural context of the client's life and experience
3. The client's most important needs at a moment in time
4. How much time is available to initiate change
5. What objectives and goals have been agreed on
6. The preferences, style, and mood of the helper
7. The philosophy of the organization

A number of research studies have highlighted discrepancies between what helpers say they are doing in their sessions (their espoused theory) versus what they are actually doing behind closed doors. Most practitioners are far more flexible, adaptable, and pragmatic than the impression they might portray as holding allegiance to a single model. The situation is further complicated by the number of conferences held during the past years in which the major theorists appear on panels together, often borrowing ideas from one another. The boundaries between theories are becoming increasingly blurred.

Common Ingredients

Another way of looking at the theories is that instead of picking and sorting through the various options to select the best treatment option that each one has to offer, we should look at what all of them have in common. In other words, at first (or even fourth) glance, the various theories appear to be diametrically opposed to one another in a number of dimensions:

- Whether focus is on the past, present, or future
- Whether they believe that people are essentially good, bad, or neutral
- Whether the client is primarily responsible for the way things go, the counselor is in charge, or the role is shared equally
- Whether the emphasis is on insight, action, or a combination of both
- Whether attention is given to thoughts, feelings, or behavior
- Whether the counselor's role is an expert, consultant, or friend
- Whether the content, process, or specific goals are given priority

In spite of all these differences between theories that make them seem irreconcilable, if not absurdly contradictory, they actually do have more in common than their inventors would pretend. Think about it: How can it really be possible to help someone doing what a cognitive helper does (confronting irrational beliefs) when a gestalt, narrative, or reality practitioner might be equally effective doing something apparently very different?

What if, however, the various theories are not really that different after all, especially in their actual practice? It so happens that most of the theories previously reviewed subscribe to some concepts (or at least use them behind closed doors) that are fairly universal, even across cultures. A *curandero* (witch doctor) in Peru, a psychologist in Iowa, a hypnotherapist in France, a healer in Ghana, a teacher in Montreal, a nurse in Manhattan, or a family therapist in Singapore all employ similar variables in their work.

This should be very exciting news for you. It means that even though you do not have to memorize all the theories in the field, there are a few variables you should become very familiar with. Regardless of where and how you practice, with whom you choose to work, and what style you develop as your very own, you are likely to use the following ingredients:

- *Hope.* Planting positive expectations in others' minds so they are favorably disposed toward the help you are offering.
- *Altered states.* Creating a state of "hyper-suggestibility" in which people are more open than usual to new ideas.
- *Catharsis.* The release of pent-up thoughts and feelings.
- *Helping relationship.* An alliance constructed that creates an environment conducive to trust, disclosure, and experimentation.
- *Reinforcement.* The application of support and rewards to encourage further movement and action.
- *Rehearsal.* Opportunities to practice new behaviors and receive feedback.
- *Alternative reality.* New perceptions of experiences or situations that are more empowering and constructive.
- *Task facilitation.* Structures for applying what was learned in sessions to the outside world.
- *Feedback.* Soliciting feedback from clients about their satisfaction with helping and evaluating outcomes to make needed adjustments.

Conclusions About Theory

Based on the theories we have explored in this chapter, the following conclusions may be reached:

1. Development is progressive, sequential, predictable, and cyclical.

2. Cultural variations in behavior make generalizations challenging.

3. Variations *within* groups may sometimes be greater than those *between* groups.

4. People are thinking, feeling, and behaving beings.

5. Every theory has some contributions and limitations to consider.

6. Rather than focusing on how each theory is different, it is more useful to look at how they are similar.

The Bottom Line

Someone is sitting in front of you, obviously in great pain. He is doing his best to control his feelings, but you can see tears forming in his eyes and his nails digging into the palms of his hands. His voice vibrates when he speaks, and you are trying to concentrate on what he is telling you, which so far does not make a lot of sense. Finally, he shrugs, as if to say that even he isn't sure what he means. But the fact remains that this is a desperate man. He is looking to you for help. He believes that you can save his life.

Where are your theories now that you need them? Somewhere, somehow, you are going to have to do something. The man is waiting, eagerly and impatiently. Your mind races, sorting through the options you have. The problem is that there are too many choices. You take a deep breath and try and relax. Back to basics. The bottom line.

There are three questions that you want to answer:

1. Where are you going?

2. How will you get there?

3. How will you know when you arrive?

To answer these questions, you will need to draw on some theories to explain what is going on with this man and what you believe should be the focus of treatment. Keep in mind that each theory you consult will likely focus on a different facet of his experience. Some practitioners might address his depression and recommend medication. Others would see him as emotionally restricted and in need of support. Still others would address the underlying helplessness he feels.

Before you drive yourself crazy running around in circles, consider that it probably does not matter nearly as much as you think where you start. Pick an approach, any approach, as long as you feel reasonably competent in its execution and it is appropriate for your client population. If this model does not work, meaning it does not produce positive outcomes consistent with the negotiated goals, you will need to make adjustments and perhaps even select another framework from which to operate. You would be surprised how often even experienced practitioners persist in using their favorite theory over and over with a particular client when it is not useful in the situation.

As a beginner, you will be working under supervision. You will have other experts review your plan and question your intentions. You must have a rationale for what you do in sessions; it is not sufficient to "trust your intuition," because such instincts are the result of experience you haven't accumulated yet.

Remember: Theory is your friend. It is the place to start when you are trying to sort out a complex, confusing situation. The man, your client, is still waiting. He looks at you for help. What will you do?

This discussion will be continued in the next chapter on the process and stages of counseling. Regardless of your theoretical allegiance, there is a generic model for helping people that follows a similar sequential process.

For Review

- Theories help you sort and organize information, provide a framework for planning and intervention, and assess the effect of helping efforts.
- All helpers operate from a theory that guides their behavior, even though they operate eclectically, using interventions from many approaches.
- It is desirable for beginners to concentrate on one theoretical model that is well-suited for the setting, clients, and parameters that are available.
- People develop naturally in a relatively orderly fashion, sometimes cycling back through stages during times of transition and crisis. Your job is to help support, stimulate, and guide people through those stages.
- Learning theories provide you with an understanding of what inhibits and encourages the development of new understanding and behavior. No single theory captures all the variables and influences involved.
- Theories of intervention place different emphases on the helper's role, client's responsibilities, focus for exploration, and so on. In spite of these differences, there are universal factors that operate in most approaches, including a relationship designed to be supportive and influential, opportunities to practice new behavior, and altered perceptions of one's situation.

For Reflection and Practice

1. Make a list of five ideas, concepts, or terms that you found most confusing in this chapter. Make a commitment to research further what they mean by consulting the suggested readings, asking your instructor, or talking to your classmates.

2. Form a discussion group to share ideas with your classmates about your different ideas about how change occurs. Talk to each other about your most significant learning experiences, then try to find common themes that were most influential in your changes.

3. Reflect on where you are functioning developmentally in your life right now. What are some of the major tasks that are most appropriate for someone of your age, gender, culture, and situation?

4. Interview several helpers about which theories they use to guide their practice. Find out how each one settled on a particular model.

5. Write about how you think people grow, learn, and change best. In your theory, talk about what you believe helps people the most.

For Further Reading

Corey, G. (2005). *Theory and practice of counseling and psychotherapy* (7th ed.). Belmont, CA: Wadsworth.

Corsini, R. J. (2008). *Current psychotherapies* (8th ed.). Belmont, CA: Wadsworth.

Halbur, D. A., & Halbur, K. V. (2006). *Developing your theoretical orientation in counseling and psychotherapy.* Boston: Pearson.

Ivey, A. E., D'Andrea, M., Ivey, M., & Simek-Morgan, L. (2007). *Theories of counseling and psychotherapy: A multicultural perspective* (6th ed.). Boston: Allyn and Bacon.

O'Brien, M., & Houston, G. (2007). *Integrative therapy: A practitioner's guide* (2nd ed.). Thousand Oaks, CA: Sage.

Sharf, R. S. (2008). *Theories of psychotherapy and counseling: Concepts and cases* (4th ed.). Belmont, CA: Wadsworth.

3

Processes and Stages

I f you found all the different approaches to help people a bit overwhelming, relief is on the way. Although it is true that there are dozens of helping methods you might employ, all of which have their enthusiastic followers, there is really a generic framework for doing this sort of work. Regardless of the setting, client population, professional affiliation, or personality style, most practitioners subscribe to a generic process that follows similar stages.

In its simplest form, helping has a beginning, a middle, and an end. There are a lot of different names for these stages, and certainly a variety of distinct processes that are emphasized by different approaches, but for now we will consider a model that will get you started. This combines several features of those you reviewed briefly in the previous chapter. It is existential and constructivist in the sense that it looks at a person's concept of personal meaning. It is influenced a bit by the psychoanalytic approach, in that there is some attention to influences from the past. There is something of reality therapy integrated, in that the client is encouraged to look at personal choices and their consequences. There are also components from the cognitive and Adlerian approaches, because clients are asked to examine the internal thinking that results in their external behavior. Finally, there is a strong humanistic thread in the emphasis on establishing a supportive relationship and attending to a person's underlying feelings, and in the belief that people have the capacity to initiate their own growth, with a little help along the way.

Because you may not remember or understand the differences between these various theories just yet, rest assured that they (and others you will learn) all contribute something to an integrated model of intervention.

Stages of Helping

You are already familiar with some of the stages of helping because they basically follow the logical progression of any learning process: First, you define where you want to go, then you explore the territory, figure out what you have discovered, and integrate this new learning into your future actions. When someone consults you for help, you will basically undertake a journey that corresponds to these stages (see Table 3.1).

Table 3.1   Stages of Helping Process With Corresponding Helping Skills

Stage	Skills
Pretreatment	Planting positive expectations Preparing for readiness to change
Exploration	Paraphrasing Reflecting feelings Probing, asking open-ended questions Building alliances, communicating empathy
Promoting insight	Interpreting Challenging Reflecting thoughts and feelings Confronting
Action	Goal setting Decision making Reinforcing progress Negotiating homework
Evaluation	Summarizing Supporting Identifying unfinished business Planning for setbacks

Like any transformative trip, preparations begin long before the embarkation point. You do some reading first. You talk to others who have been where you venture to go. You make some preliminary decisions about priorities and significant sites. You plan a bit about your itinerary. Sometimes you hire an experienced guide to show you the way.

Stage 1: Pretreatment

Helping begins long before a person ever seeks professional help. People rarely choose professional help as a first choice, or even a second or third.

It is time consuming, inconvenient, expensive, and embarrassing. For these reasons, by the time you ever see people for help, they will have already exhausted almost every other strategy that comes to mind.

There is some set of symptoms that are experienced as annoying or perhaps even debilitating. The person is uncomfortable, sometimes desperate, but always impatient to find some answers. He comes with a particular frame of mind and expectations. He has decided to seek help at this particular time for some reason. Why now? What is he looking for? What sense does he make of what is going on? What has he tried already that hasn't worked?

These are just a few of the questions you will wish to consider during this pretreatment stage. Of course, you have not met your client yet, but no matter: She is definitely thinking about you. She is planning what she will say and how she will frame it. She is wondering if you will judge her critically. She wants you to like her, to approve of her. Most of all, she hopes that you can be of assistance.

The pretreatment stage can be so intense, the symptoms so bothersome, and the client's motivation and commitment so focused, that sometimes there is little that you have to do; most of the hard work has already been set in motion. There are a number of instances when even a single session is enough to act as a catalyst for the thinking and actions already begun. Your main job at this early stage is to plant favorable expectations during initial phone contact and help prepare the person for a commitment to change, working hard to make that happen.

Stage 2: Exploration

Naturally, the first place to start is to hear the client's story. What is the problem? What do you think that means? What does the person expect from you? What background information do you need to understand this person and the context for what has been going on?

This doesn't mean that you are acting as an interrogator. Quite the opposite, actually: You are doing your best to create a solid relationship in which the person feels heard, respected, honored, and understood. Sometimes, this is more than enough on its own to produce miraculous results. Although this stage is certainly focused on gathering information, another significant task is to begin building a solid alliance with the client (described in the next chapter).

Your job is to find out what is going on. You want to know the context for the present symptoms. You are interested in relevant history. You need to understand the unique culture of the person, including influences of gender, race, religion, socioeconomic class, and other such variables. But this exploration is not about what *you* need to know. Rather, what you are doing is helping the client to explore the nature of the issues.

Depending on your theoretical orientation, you may concentrate primarily on the past, spending many months covering personal history from birth until the present moment. If time is limited and you have only a single half hour to make a difference, then an abbreviated exploration will hone in on relevant information that allows you to formulate a treatment plan.

Almost all practitioners would agree that some sort of exploration is needed to study the situation, collect information, and formulate a diagnosis. Imagine, for example, that someone consults you with a problem related to family members. What immediately comes to mind that you would want to know before you could help this person?

You would probably want to know exactly what she means by "family members." Who specifically is she referring to?

"Just that nobody seems to get along," she explains, even though you still don't understand what she is talking about.

Not only will you want to tease that out a bit, you will also need to know who is in her family. Has she had this sort of problem previously? Remembering the pretreatment stage, you remember to ask her about what she's tried before to solve things. You wonder what has worked and what hasn't.

Then you realize that this single family conflict doesn't define her whole life. You want to know about how she spends a typical day. Who is she close to? What does she do for work? How does she spend her leisure time?

Recalling something about developmental theory, you also want to know a few things about her life growing up. What were the significant events that stand out? What did she struggle with the most?

I could go on and on and on. In fact, some helpers do spend years just in this exploration stage. Before you scoff at this, remember that it would take almost all the time you have left to bring any individual up to date on everything you have experienced before. Whereas, once upon a time, psychoanalytic practitioners (remember Sigmund Freud and company?) scheduled three to four sessions per week, for a minimum of five years, just to cover all the material, nowadays things are considerably shortened to a matter of months or weeks.

It is usual and customary to spend somewhere between the first session (called "intake interview") and a half-dozen sessions completing this stage in the process. It really is a matter of time and resources available. Ideally, of course, you would love the luxury of spending several months getting to know someone before you would ever be so presumptuous as to offer any thoughtful response. Alas, you probably won't have that sort of time, so you must learn to conduct your exploration efficiently and systematically.

Even in a matter of minutes, you would be surprised how much you can learn from someone who is being even marginally cooperative. During this assessment process, you are also concentrating on building as much rapport and trust with the person as you can.

You are doing everything you can to establish yourself as an expert in the person's eyes. You want to plant favorable expectations that you know what you are doing and that you can, indeed, be of assistance. The end of this stage, and transition to the next one, sounds something like this:

> You have revealed a lot about yourself in the time we have been together. You've told me a lot about what is going on in your life. I also appreciate your frankness in telling me what you hope I can do for you.
>
> Although I've just met you, it seems to me that the original problem you presented is only part of what brought you to ask for help. You have mentioned a number of other related concerns that you'd also like to explore.
>
> Before I tell you what I think is going on and what I propose to do to help, I want you to know that what you are going through is a normal part of adjustment, and I am fairly certain that you can make rapid progress. Of course, much depends on how hard you are willing to work and how fast you want this to go.

If this sounds like some sort of a motivational speech, you aren't far wrong. It is critical that you provide the client, even during the first contact, with some sort of feedback about what you have heard and what you understand. More than that, however, you've got to provide some hope.

The object of any first session is to get the person to come back for a second session; if you can't do that, you can't help most people. So your goals during this stage are twofold: One, collect as much information as you can, and two, capture the client's interest so that future helping can continue. Both of these goals link together rather nicely, resulting in some preliminary understanding that can next be pursued further.

Stage 3: Insight

You will remember that some theories of helping are primarily insight oriented, whereas others consider themselves as action-focused treatments. Examples of the former include theories such as psychoanalytic, existential, and humanistic approaches, whereas the latter group is identified with behavioral, strategic, and problem-solving approaches. Of course, others, such as cognitive, narrative, Adlerian, and reality theories, combine features of both. In other words, insight is treated very differently by various practitioners. Some believe it should be the major emphasis of all helping efforts, whereas others think that it is a luxury that is often not needed. Whether action-oriented helpers acknowledge it or not, they still spend brief periods of time helping people understand how they got themselves in trouble.

Unconscious Desires

One type of insight that might be most familiar to you is the approach taken by psychoanalytic theory. It is believed that the problems we have today result, in part, from unresolved issues of the past. Sounds reasonable, doesn't it? It makes sense that there are thoughts, feelings, urges, instincts, rumblings, and images of which we are not fully aware. Nevertheless, these internal forces affect us in ways that are sometimes unrecognized.

One person might find himself repeatedly stuck in the same sorts of romantic entanglements that are unsatisfying and dysfunctional, even if they offer a degree of familiarity, that he observed in his own parents' relationship. Another person keeps trying to prove herself over and over, continuously pushing herself to higher levels of achievement. What she does not realize is that her drive comes primarily from competition she is feeling with her sister. Still another example involves a student who learns helping skills, not only because she wants to help people, but because she wants to feed her need for others to depend on her.

In each of these cases, and many others, the goal is to help people to uncover their unconscious desires and drives. It is believed that once you become aware of what you are doing, you can exercise more control over your behavior. Rather than being driven by motives beyond awareness, insight into such patterns allows people to make new choices.

Secondary Gains

Another type of insight was spawned through the perceptive observations of nurses who noticed that patients recovering from surgery and medical ailments were not recovering as quickly as they should have been. Even though their bodies were responding to the medication or procedure, for some reason, these individuals reported they were still not feeling much better. They seemed to enjoy remaining in a sick role. They seemed to derive "secondary gains" as a result of their illness.

So, you might wonder, whatever could possibly be good about remaining sick? Think about it. Better yet, make a list in your head of all the benefits and payoffs that might be enjoyed by someone who does not get better:

- You get sympathy.
- You get to feel sorry for yourself and feel helpless so you do not have to do anything constructive.

- You can control powerful others, like doctors and family members, who will be frustrated by your lack of improvement in spite of their best efforts.
- You can be in a bad mood and lash out at others according to your whims. Afterward, you can apologize and be forgiven: After all, you are sick so you can't help it.
- You can take a "time out" from your life and have others take care of you.

This is just a short list of possibilities. There are actually many other secondary gains that are possible, and not just with being physically sick but with any sort of psychological problem as well. What this means is that you can help people generate some degree of insight into what they are getting out of their dysfunctional behavior. Because the pattern wouldn't persist unless some benefit was derived, the key is to uncover what purpose is being served.

Most problems that people present—whether excessive guilt, self-loathing, dependence, addiction, or anything else—often have the following payoffs:

1. They represent a form of control in which the behavior somehow manipulates others.

2. They can function as a kind of self-punishment to pay for perceived wrongs. They wipe the slate clean so that the individual is allowed to continue doing the same things over and over ("Do you think I *like* being this way? Look how I'm suffering!").

3. They work as an effective distraction. As long as you are preoccupied with the problem, you can procrastinate and hide, avoiding dealing with other things in life that are more threatening and even more painful.

4. They help the person avoid responsibility. Often you will hear the refrain, "I can't help it!" or "It's not my fault." The self-defeating behavior acts as a scapegoat to help the person remain stuck.

The object lesson of bringing secondary gains into awareness is similar to what the psychoanalyst does, but instead of looking at the past, you are examining the present. Once you are aware of the games you are playing with yourself and others, you can't get away with them anymore. The idea is to ruin the pleasure that is possible when operating from blissful ignorance.

Irrational Assumptions

One of the contributions of the cognitive therapies is the attention that is drawn to the ways that certain thinking processes lead to negative emotional reactions. The strategy with this kind of insight is to confront people with the ways that they are causing their own misery by the ways they are choosing to interpret reality.

In narrative therapy and other constructivist approaches, people are helped to realize that the stories they have adopted as true representations of their experience may, in fact, be the result of ways they have been indoctrinated by others. The act of realizing that you can create an alternative version of the same events, one that is more consistent with your own values and culture, is indeed an empowering insight.

Examples of irrational beliefs that are confronted by a more cognitive style include the following:

1. The idea that things are not nearly as bad as they are made out to be. You are most likely exaggerating the extent of the problem, as well as the extent to which it controls you.

2. The notion that the world is fair and that you should get exactly what you deserve. In fact, you are not nearly as important as you think and the world does not conspire to make your life miserable.

3. Demands made of yourself, and others, that things should be a certain way. This is another way that people inflate their sense of power and believe that the world should live up to their expectations. When things go differently, the result is tragic, rather than only mildly disappointing.

4. The belief that other people and external events can make you feel a particular way, without your consent. According to this insight approach, everything that you feel, and however you react, is based primarily on your perceptions and interpretations of what has happened. If you do not like the way you are feeling, just change the way you are viewing the situation.

Discrepant Behavior

Another kind of insight that might be generated in this stage involves confronting people with inconsistencies in their behavior. Whether in a group, family, or individual session, the individual may be encouraged to look at discrepancies between

- Behavior now versus actions in the past: "You say that you are feeling discouraged about progress you are making, but I notice that just now you challenged me in ways that you never would have before. You also just finished telling a story about how you are now so much more assertive at work than you could have imagined."
- Things said now versus things said previously: "I'm confused. You say that you don't love your mother, but I've heard you say before that she's one of the most important people in the world to you."

- Things said versus observable behavior: "You describe yourself as passive and a pushover, but you just strongly disagreed with me. How could someone do that, if she were really the way you described yourself?"

This type of confrontive insight, favored by practitioners with a more active, directive style, is intended to push people to look at themselves in new ways. Like all other forms that have been briefly reviewed, the plan of this approach is based on the assumption that bringing hidden patterns into awareness forces people to change the ways they act in the future.

Underlying Feelings

If the preceding approaches focus on internal thoughts or behavioral patterns, another kind of insight favored by humanistic practitioners uncovers repressed or unacknowledged feelings. The intention here is to reflect back to the individual what you hear, see, sense, and feel is being expressed beneath the surface.

A fellow student says to you after class, "Excuse me, but did this stuff make sense to you today?"

If you were to treat this question as a surface inquiry, you would answer concretely, saying something like, "Yes, it did," or "No, it didn't." End of story.

If, on the other hand, you attempted to decode what is really being expressed by this inquiry, you would not hear it as a question at all, but rather as a statement of intense feeling. You might, for example, respond as follows: "You're feeling apprehensive about the material because it seemed confusing to you."

Of course, this may or may not be an accurate reflection of what the person is feeling. That hardly matters as much as the intention to help the person clarify what he or she is really feeling. The assumption behind this kind of insight is that, eventually, the person will reach a degree of understanding about his or her own internal states that will be sufficient for him or her to resolve the problem.

In theory, anyway, Carl Rogers believed that insights such as this would promote lasting changes in someone's life. Although it is true that reflecting feelings, or any other form of insight work, may be enough to help someone significantly, it is not often sufficient to maintain the momentum without other structures and support systems in place. Indeed, there are people who aren't so much interested in change as they are understanding themselves better. For many others, however, insight is a desirable stage in the process, maybe even a necessary one, but it is often not enough.

Table 3.2   Some Types of Insight

Insight	Theoretical Origins	Example
Unconscious	Psychoanalytic	"I react with such rage toward my teacher because she reminds me of my mean aunt."
Secondary gains	Behavioral	"I complain a lot because I get a lot of attention and pity from others."
Social	Narrative	"I defer to men because that is the role construction I learned from media and family members growing up. It is also part of my Latina culture."
Irrational beliefs	Cognitive	"I am so upset because I am exaggerating how important this incident is."
Systemic	Structural	"I am the one designated in my family as the 'problem' to distract others from their own conflicts."
Discrepancies	Various	"I call myself shy but I realize there are times when I do act assertively, like right now when I disagreed with you."
Affect	Client-centered	"I'm really proud of what I did, although I've never admitted that before."
Polarity	Gestalt	"I have two parts of me, one that wants out of this relationship, one that wants to remain."

You know more than a few people walking around who have perfect insight into their motives, but they still do the same crazy things over and over. You know folks who understand only too well why they keep getting themselves into the same predicaments, yet they still follow the same patterns, apparently helpless to act on what they supposedly understand. You might even be able to think of a few aspects of your own life where you have perfect clarity about what you should do or what you need to do, but you still do not do it.

With the vast majority of the people you try to help, the insights that you generate, whether they involve uncovering unconscious desires, irrational beliefs, unexpressed feelings, or secondary gains, will still need to be translated into constructive action. If you have not yet encountered resistance to your efforts, you may very well see it here.

People say they want to change, but basically, they want others to do the work. Generally, change involves so much discomfort, adjustment, hard work, and pain that people will exhaust every other option first. They will try to blame others. They will wallow in self-pity. They will appear helpless so they can get others to do the work. Once they have reached a point of desperation, or at least great discomfort, then they will act. Expect this. Don't take it personally. Your job in promoting insight is to help the person to feel more miserable with the way he or she is; then he or she will be motivated to do something about it.

Stage 4: Action

The transition from insight to action is a difficult one; this is when you lose people if you don't handle this carefully. People are often frightened of the unknown. They don't want to be responsible for their own happiness. If it's not more fun, then it's at least more comfortable and familiar to feel helpless enough that you can't do anything about your situation. That is why people stay in miserable situations, abusive relationships, and dysfunctional patterns: They may not be the best thing in the world but at least they are familiar. People can get used to most anything. Besides, they reason that the unknown could be even worse.

In the action stage, you are helping people convert what they now understand about themselves into some specific, constructive steps that will make their lives better. Like any problem-solving strategy, you would likely undertake the following:

1. *Establish goals.* In light of what has been learned, specify objectives that are to be reached.

2. *Take inventory.* Make a list of things that have already been tried and have not worked so you don't waste time repeating them.

3. *Generate alternatives.* Brainstorm an exhaustive list of options that might be attempted.

4. *Narrow the options.* Select a first-choice plan, or create one that combines the best features of what was generated.

5. *Rehearse.* Practice scenarios that might unfold; role play new situations; practice new skills or strategies that could be used.

6. *Give feedback.* Critique and process what was learned from the previous steps; refine the plan in light of new adjustments.

7. *Give homework.* Try whatever was agreed on in the real world.

It is not uncommon for helpers to tell people that what they do in sessions is not nearly as important as what they do outside of sessions, in their lives, where it really counts. Rarely do things work out as planned the first time. However, if you have built a foundation through the previous stages, then you have earned the trust, confidence, and most of all, patience of the client, so you have the time to experiment with several different plans until you create the right combination of factors.

Stage 5: Evaluation

The last stage is one in which you assess, with the person you are helping, the extent to which desired goals were reached. To what extent were the presenting complaints reduced or eliminated? What more needs to be done? How can the person generalize what was learned to other areas of life? These are not questions that you necessarily wait until the end of treatment to ask; at any stage of the process you can—and should—find out how you are doing. After every few sessions, it is a good idea to ask the client directly what you are doing that is most and least helpful.

In today's professional climate, helpers are called on more and more to demonstrate that they have truly made a difference. You will be asked to document what you did and what resulted from these efforts. You may be asked to justify to third parties (funding agencies, insurance companies, referrals, etc.) that what you are offering is indeed a worthwhile enterprise. You will be forced to evaluate whether what you did in your helping efforts was indeed effective.

This emphasis on accountability is a mixed blessing. On one hand, there is a lot of annoying, time-consuming paperwork. It also doesn't feel very good to have to spend so much time justifying your existence and defending your actions. On the other hand, however, the evaluative process is what makes you a better helper in the future. It forces you to think through exactly what you did and measure what effects occurred. This allows you to be more systematic in your efforts to improve and grow as a helper. You collect more and more data about what works best in which circumstances. You learn about what you can do, and what you can't do, in various situations. Finally, the evaluative process makes you accountable and cautious—important conditions to protect the safety of those who are entrusting their lives in your care.

Closure Issues

One of the distinct limitations of any helping effort is to make the changes last long after the interventions are over. So often, people initiate new plans—to become more assertive or less shy, to lose weight, to stop smoking, to make more friends, to reduce alcohol consumption, to change jobs or relationships—only to find that when the supportive helping relationship ends, a relapse occurs.

Closure issues are so critical in helping efforts because you do everything you can to ensure that the changes "stick." Your strategy during this final stage is not only to summarize the gains that have been made and to offer needed support, but also to take whatever steps are indicated to keep the momentum going after the sessions have ceased.

Most often, closure involves taking care of the following steps:

- *Talk about reactions to the ending.* Acknowledge that it is time to move on. Invite the client to talk about relevant thoughts and feelings.
- *Deal with unfinished business.* Even if there is not time to complete all the work left to do, you can still identify areas for future progress.
- *Review what was accomplished.* Ask the client to summarize what occurred, what was learned, and where things are going next. Then fill in what was left out.
- *Make plans for the future.* Structure future homework assignments that are designed to be self-monitored.
- *Talk about support.* Build alternative support systems that will encourage future progress. Include things like support groups and structured rituals.
- *Plan for a relapse.* Without being unduly pessimistic, remind your client that setbacks are inevitable and, furthermore, that they are no big deal. Make a strong case for applying what was learned to deal with any regression or disappointments.
- *Make plans for follow up.* Even if only a phone call is used, make arrangements to check in at various intervals to reinforce progress, offer continued support, and provide "booster" sessions as needed.
- *Say goodbye.* Let go in such a way that the client feels encouraged and empowered. Acknowledge the ambivalence about saying goodbye. Launch the person into the world with optimism about the future.

For Review

- Helping efforts usually proceed along a series of stages involving the (a) decision to seek help, (b) assessment of presenting problems, (c) exploration of relevant issues and background, (d) understanding and insight related to how a problem evolved and why it persists, (e) rehearsal and practice of new behavior, and (f) assessment of outcomes.
- The helping process begins long before the client seeks help. Find out what was attempted previously to solve the problem.
- The various kinds of insight that may be promoted will vary, depending on time available and the client's particular needs.

- When time is available, the best helping efforts involve both promoting understanding and offering constructive action.
- Resistance to change is a normal part of the helping process. People are doing their best to protect themselves against perceived threats.

For Reflection and Practice

1. Look at a change effort that you are going through right now. What stage of this process are you in?

2. Talk to several individuals who are now involved in a helping relationship, and ask them about the processes and stages they are experiencing.

3. Review a time in your life that you were helped. Follow the progression of stages described in this chapter to plot your own journey.

4. Practice doing an assessment and intake interview with a partner in which you take a half hour to collect all the information you can. Review with your partner afterward what you missed and could have done differently.

5. Think about some dysfunctional behavior that you engage in, even though it does not appear to be all that helpful to you. What are some of the payoffs you enjoy as a result?

6. Because stages of evolution apply to all growth and change situations, examine your own process of learning helping skills in your class. Talk to classmates (and your instructor) about the stages of development that you are going through.

For Further Reading

Cochran, J. L., & Cochran, N. H. (2006). *The heart of counseling: A guide to developing therapeutic relationships*. Belmont, CA: Wadsworth.

Corey, M. S., & Corey, G. (2007). *Becoming a helper* (5th ed.). Belmont, CA: Wadsworth.

Egan, G. (2006). *Essentials of skilled helping*. Belmont, CA: Wadsworth.

Gazda, G. M., et al. (2005). *Human relations development: A manual for educators* (7th ed.). Boston: Allyn & Bacon.

Hutchinson, D. (2007). *The essential counselor: Process, skills, and techniques*. Boston: Lahaska Press.

Kottler, J. A., & Carlson, J. (2005). *Their finest hour: Master therapists share their greatest success stories*. Boston: Allyn & Bacon.

Neukrug, E. S., & Schwitzer, A. M. (2006). *Skills and tools for today's counselors and psychologists*. Belmont, CA: Wadsworth.

Weinberg, G. (1992). *Nearer to the heart's desire: Tales of psychotherapy*. New York: Plume.

Welfel, E. R., & Patterson, L. E. (2005). *The counseling process: A multitheoretical integrative approach* (6th ed.). Belmont, CA: Wadsworth.

4

Helping Relationships

No matter how you end up helping people, where you do it, and what form your assistance takes, it is the relationship you construct that will empower any of your interventions. This is one way in which helping skills alone do not fit, because the uniquely human connection that develops is beyond a bunch of things you *do*; it involves the way you *are* with people—your sense of *being with* people during their times of greatest need.

Reflect Back

A good way to start is by reflecting on a time in your life when you were helped tremendously by someone. This may have been a teacher, a friend or acquaintance, or perhaps a relative. Think about what it was about this relationship that made the most difference to you. It probably was not the result of any single thing that was said or done; rather, there was some cumulative effect that developed from the time you spent together.

It is likely this relationship was so influential in your life because it had certain qualities that are somewhat universal in all helping encounters. Compare your experience with the following characteristics:

You felt trust and safety. Beyond all else, the best relationships are those in which you don't feel judged and in which you can say whatever you want and know that although your behavior may be evaluated, you—as a person—will never be criticized. This sort of safety is crucial for risks to take place, the kind in which you are willing to experiment with new ways of thinking and acting.

You felt heard and understood. In so many cases, there is little that can actually be done at the time. The most important element, therefore, is to create a forum in which deep-level exploration and self-expression are possible. It feels so good to know that you aren't alone, to know that there is someone walking with you along the way. No matter what happens or how things turn out, you know that someone else understands what you are going through.

You were valued and respected. Disagreement is not only common in good helping relationships, but necessary. Nevertheless, you felt supported, perhaps even loved. This essential caring goes a long way to bolster your spirit. There comes a time when you think to yourself, "Gee, I never thought much of myself. But this person who appears so competent and wise thinks I'm okay, so maybe, just maybe, I am worth more than I thought."

You were confronted. Honesty is critical in any helping relationship. It is so rare that you ever hear the truth about the ways you are perceived by others. Such confrontations might not even involve direct feedback but rather the opportunity to look at yourself more clearly and to face the consequences of your choices.

Your needs were addressed. In helping relationships, the client is always more important. This is so different from what most people are accustomed to when there is competition over whose needs will be met first. Ultimately, the true test of whether the relationship worked or not is whether you got what you wanted, or at least what you needed. Keep in mind that what people say they desire isn't necessarily in their best interests.

Adjustments were made according to your changing needs. Things change. Constantly. The most satisfying relationships are those in which your particular moods, needs, interests, and preferences are recognized and responded to—as they evolve. What works one day may not work another. It is absolutely critical for the helper to continually assess how things are going, to find out what is optimal in any given moment, and then to customize an approach that fits best with the situation.

This list of relationship variables is hardly exhaustive. There may very well have been other factors operating that were most helpful to you. At this point, the specifics are less important than the realization that the techniques and strategies you employ mean nothing if they aren't embedded in a solid relationship with those you help.

In some cases, it may even be the relationship alone that becomes most healing. It is actually so rare in life that people feel honored and cherished and that they are understood. Beyond anything else you do for people, if you can create such an alliance and maintain it over time, you have provided a wonderful gift that can have powerful effects.

Uses of the Helping Relationship

Relationships have value far beyond providing general support. They can be used in a number of different ways, depending on what is needed. That is why, in addition to mastering any specific skills, techniques, and strategies, you must become a relationship expert. You will do this by developing just the sort of alliance that will work best for people at particular times in their lives. For someone recovering from surgery, a sympathetic relationship may be indicated. For someone in the throes of grief, or who has gotten himself in trouble, or who is feeling sorry for herself, another structure may be needed.

Diagnostic Aid

It is helpful to assume that however someone is with you, they act in a similar manner in the outside world. This isn't completely true, of course, especially because people who want help might be on their best behavior. Still, people rely on consistent coping strategies and interpersonal styles. You can be fooled, quite easily in fact, but you will still find it useful to examine the kind of relationship you have with a person as representative of what he or she might be used to.

For example, you note that someone presents himself as passive, withdrawn, and dependent. He seems to bring out in you the need to parent him and to take care of him. You feel sorry for him; he appears so helpless. As such, you become aware that you are working awfully hard to get through to him. Moreover, the harder you work, the worse he seems to get.

Under such circumstances, it is entirely possible that what you are seeing and experiencing is part of a familiar pattern (of course, it might also be situation specific and have as much to do with you as with him, but that's another story). Your relationship becomes a kind of diagnostic tool to assess what is going on, not just in session, but in other aspects of his life that may have led him to seek help in the first place.

Unfinished Business

People will respond to you not only as you really are, but as they imagine you to be. You will remind them of others they have encountered in their lives, especially those in positions of power and authority. Serving in the role of surrogate parent or wise mentor, you will not only provide guidance, but also stir things up in ways that will unfold before your very eyes. You will notice that people become angry at you even though you're pretty sure you didn't do anything to earn their wrath. You will find others in love with you, or at least infatuated. Still others will confuse you, as a person, with someone else who you remind them of.

There will be rich opportunities to help people resolve unfinished business through the relationship that you will have constructed with them. Through patient, gentle, sometimes forceful probes, you can facilitate working through the unresolved issues.

Problem-Solving Collaboration

Once a partnership has been created, opportunities abound for working together on presenting problems. Two heads are definitely better than one, especially when your head is clear, neutral, and focused. You are able to model ways of thinking through difficulties, not to mention following through on intentions. You help people generate new options for their lives. When someone feels stuck or discouraged, then you can also help him or her to look at other possibilities. More than anything else, you help people to feel they have an advocate in their corner, someone who will be frank and honest, yet also kind and sensitive.

Novel Interaction Experience

For some people, it may be the first time in their lives they have ever had a relationship with someone who treats them kindly, supports them unconditionally, and yet confronts their game playing. In a sense, your job is to provide the kind of relationship in which it's possible for people to experience new ways of relating to others. When you challenge covert acts, uncover self-defeating patterns, and enforce clear boundaries, you are teaching people they must be held accountable for their behavior.

When someone tries to be manipulative, you label what is going on and initiate alternative ways to get needs met. When there are attempts made to withdraw, pout, or sabotage things, you step in to take things in a more healthy direction. You do everything in your power to create an ideal relationship that is open, honest, and caring—the sort of the model that will provide a blueprint for other relationships in the future.

Customized Relationships

It might sound as if each of these kinds of relationships is a relatively stable construction that remains the same throughout your encounters with a particular person. Far more likely, you will change the sort of relationship as you progress through each stage in the helping process. Furthermore, you will continuously make adjustments with each person, depending on what seems to be working best. In each case, you will take into account the person's issues, history, culture, gender, preferences, and needs. At various times, you will tinker with things to make the relationship more amenable to intimacy and trust in the beginning, goal setting and limit testing in the middle, and transference reactions and closure issues toward the end. Please remember that the kind of relationship you use is fluid, flexible, and continuously evolving.

Basically Speaking

After this review of basic concepts, it is time to look at the basics of designing sound therapeutic relationships. Keep the following guidelines in mind:

1. *Be warm and engaging.* Make yourself as accessible and approachable as possible. Your job in the beginning is to capture people's interest so they will return for future help. For that to occur, they must trust you. You don't have a lot of time to make that happen.

   build trust —

2. *Show strength and confidence.* Beyond all else, people are looking for hope, and you are there to give it to them. You want to appear poised, calm, and in control, as if you've seen it all before and know just what to do to make things better. You may not feel this way inside, but it is very important that you appear to others that you are confident and resourceful. If you are truly over your head, of course, you will wish to make a referral to someone more experienced.

   show confidence

3. *Be consistent and dependable.* Trust is built through successive tests. *Why* should the person you are helping ever believe you are trustworthy unless you can prove it through your behavior? If you do nothing else, make yourself as solid and dependable as you can. Sometimes what people are looking for the most is someone they can count on.

4. *Model honesty and integrity.* Be the kind of the person you want others to be. People will try to imitate your best features, especially if you are seen as having qualities they want for themselves. If you want others to be frank and open, then you have to present yourself in that way. This may seem at odds with the point above about showing confidence you may not always feel, but there are times when revealing your uncertainty and humanity encourages others to do the same.

5. *Restrain your personal needs.* On the one hand, you want to be as transparent and authentic as possible, because this will lead people to trust you. On

the other hand, you don't want to meet your personal needs. That's why before you do or say anything in session, you must ask yourself what you are trying to accomplish and how what you are attempting will do that. Everything that you do should be for the benefit of the person you are helping, rather than to satisfy your own curiosity or meet any of your own needs. This is a difficult challenge to master and the reason why good supervision is important to monitor your intentions and motives.

6. *Be careful with self-disclosure.* Sharing personal stories can be a very powerful method to deepen the relationship, model personal effectiveness, illustrate some idea or concept, and show transparency and authenticity. However, for beginners, it can also be perceived by clients as self-indulgent. As a general rule, you want to avoid using examples from your own life unless you can't think of another way to get the point across. If you do disclose something personal from your own life, be as brief as possible; every moment you are talking about yourself is a moment that detracts from the client's own experience.

7. *Resonate with what you sense going on.* Use your eyes, ears, and your intuition to read what is going on. What is your client feeling? What is he or she thinking inside? What is happening between you at any moment in time? What does he or she really mean by the statement just expressed? What is the hidden agenda? What is left unexpressed?

   Pure empathy means you are crawling inside someone else. As best as is humanly possible, you want to know about another's personal experience. You want to feel what it is like to be that other person. From such a stance, you will find it much easier to reflect accurately what you sense is going on.

8. *Go with the flow.* Things change very quickly. Helpers get in trouble when they insist on staying with an agenda that has already become obsolete. Monitor what is going on. Ask yourself if you like what is happening; if not, change the way you are doing things; create a different sort of relationship and see how that one works.

9. *Stay flexible.* Keep in mind the way cultural and gender differences strongly influence the ways that people respond to kinds of relationships. Depending on the background and experience of each person, you will need to adjust the ways you work.

10. *Respond therapeutically.* You have a hundred, maybe a thousand, different response options at any moment. You will also drive yourself crazy if you try to guess which is the right one. In fact, there are often a dozen different strategies that may all be appropriate. Sometimes, you can't even tell in retrospect which was the best path to take. In the face of such uncertainty, keep in mind that even if you don't help someone, you don't want to hurt him or her. Ask yourself what is needed at this moment. Go with what comes to

mind. Evaluate the results. Make adjustments as needed, or make new choices. If you have built a good relationship, then you have lots of room for mistakes and misjudgments. Your client will forgive you for the error of your ways if you have laid a foundation of mutual trust. In some cases, it is even therapeutic to admit you made a mistake so the client can see you aren't infallible. Any single intervention matters less than the bigger picture you have helped to create.

11. *Show the person that you care.* I saved the most important point for last. Prove that you understood what the person is communicating by responding back in an empathic manner. Use everything in your power to demonstrate your level of caring and commitment to being helpful.

Practical Issues

Before we talk about what to do with someone you are helping, it is first important to understand the context for this relationship. Helping relationships are not like other kinds of conversations or social interactions. One of the things that makes them so magical is that they appear to exist in another dimension of reality, one that it is free from distractions and interruptions.

Wherever it is that you intend to help someone, you want to make certain that you have a quiet space that is free from all intrusions and interruptions. Because you are communicating to this person that he or she is the most important person in the world to you at that moment in time and that you are devoting all your attention and energy toward this endeavor, then you want to make sure that the setting is most conducive to this.

What does this mean specifically? It means arranging the space so you are sitting a comfortable distance apart, not too far away, but also not too close. You never want to sit behind a desk or have a large object standing between you and the other person. During the time you are together, do not answer the phone, do not tolerate any interruptions (unless an absolute emergency), and give the person your full and complete attention.

It is a good idea to arrange the space so you are facing one another, but perhaps at a slight angle so that one can comfortably look away. Be respectful of cultural differences among the people you help, such as how eye contact, nonverbal behavior, and forms of address are different.

Getting the Relationship Started

Let's get even more specific as to what you need to do to build constructive relationships that are helpful to people. When I was first learning to build helping relationships, I used a checklist (more of a "cheat sheet," actually, because I kept it hidden) to remind myself of the most important things to focus my concentration (see Table 4.1).

Table 4.1   Helping Relationship Checklist

☑ Decide whom to include
☑ Eliminate distractions
☑ Focus attention
☑ Communicate warmth and caring
☑ Listen actively
☑ Assess expectations
☑ Honor the person's worldview
☑ Discuss ground rules
☑ Demystify the helping process
☑ Enter client's world
☑ Minimize questions
☑ Reflect content and feelings
☑ Slow down
☑ Work collaboratively
☑ Solicit feedback
☑ Get a commitment

Decide Whom to Include

This is a more complicated consideration than you can possibly imagine. Some professionals believe that all helping is a kind of family intervention, regardless of which people are in attendance, because when you change one person, you change the whole system that the person is part of. Other practitioners believe that as many family members and significant others as possible should be included in any helping effort. (Personally, I find this chaotic and uncontrollable.) Nevertheless, you must decide whether to speak to the person alone; to invite his or her partner, parent, or spouse; or even to include others who may be involved in the situation.

Find an Environment Free of Distractions

As much as is possible under the circumstances, create a private space where you can talk without distractions. Situate yourselves so that you can face one another fully. If more than one person is present, arrange the seating in a triangular or circular setting so that each person can address the anothers. Set things up so that once you have begun, there are no interruptions.

Give Your Undivided Attention

Don't answer the phone. Don't let others intrude. For the few minutes you are together, give your undivided attention, communicating that everything you have to give is focused on the other person during the session. Use your eyes, your face, your posture and body position, and your head nods and expressions to say unequivocally that you are listening intently to what is being said.

Focus Your Concentration

Helping is a form of meditation, in that you use all your powers to focus your concentration on a single act. Push aside distracting thoughts. Ignore your grumbling stomach or personal agenda. Forget about what is waiting for you outside the room. For just a few minutes, use every bit of your energy to hone in on everything that is going on.

Communicate Warmth

Balance your look of complete concentration with accessibility. Don't display a "shrink mask," in which you appear completely unreadable; let your humanness and warmth show through. Use head nods, verbal acknowledgments ("Uh huh," "Yeah?," "Oh"), and other nonverbal means to let the other person know that you are with him or her.

Listen Actively

There are a number of skills to be covered in the next chapter that allow you to track what is being said and prove that you truly understand. On a more general level, put yourself in a mode in which you are listening not just with your ears, but with your heart and soul. Even when you are only listening and just nodding your head, do so actively. Wait for a break, or create one if you have to, to reflect back what you heard and understand.

Find Out What the Person Expects and Desires

Before you can help people, you have to know what they are looking for. People come with very unrealistic expectations of what you can do. They think you will cure their suffering with a magic spell. They want you to take sides and agree with them. They may not think they have a problem at all, but that it is somebody else's issue.

You must know what the person has in mind so you can address discrepancies between what is expected and what can be delivered realistically. Negotiate with the person until you are both satisfied with what can be accomplished in the time parameters.

For example, a teenager wants you to straighten out his parents and teachers who are giving him a hard time. He doesn't acknowledge that he has a problem; rather, everyone else has the problem. Of course, in a sense, he is right: He is more of a problem for others than for himself. He actually enjoys the attention and power he feels from being so disruptive (see section on secondary gains in Chapter 3). Because you can't do what he wants, you find some middle ground where you both agree to find alternative ways that he can get what he wants without disrupting so many other people's lives.

Honor the Person's Worldview

Each person has a unique way in which he or she views the world. This perceptual lens is influenced by one's background and history, in particular influences from gender, culture, religion, race, socioeconomic class, and other such factors. Through intense listening, careful observations, intuitive resonance, and deep-level empathy (all honed from experience), you will collaborate with those you help to construct the ideal kind of relationship that is best suited to their needs. You would create a very different kind of relationship with an adolescent, immigrant girl than you would with an elderly man dying of a terminal illness, a victim of sexual and physical abuse, or a heroin addict. Each client views the world—and your helping efforts—differently, depending on personal experience, prior associations with helping, and unique needs and interests.

Discuss Ground Rules

Every relationship has rules, whether they are explicitly stated or not. These include, but are not limited to, assigned roles, norms for conduct, boundaries around time and place, and so on. One of the first things you will want to do is discuss the parameters of the relationship. You will need to talk about confidentiality, specifically what will happen to the things said and the conditions under which this privacy might be violated (such as if the person is a danger to himself or herself or others). You will want to discuss time limits and stick to them diligently—not only is your availability limited, but people will play games with the limits to test their power. If there are any fees involved, you will need to talk about that as well. Basically, you are telling the person what you need for the relationship to work effectively and then asking him or her to do the same.

Demystify the Helping Process

People have some very unrealistic and confusing expectations for what you can do for them. Most want you to fix them and believe that you have some sort of magic wand (or at least painless solution) to make everything better. Others will believe that you are some sort of guru with special powers. Although it is certainly true that you have a degree of training and expertise in your chosen field, helping relationships follow a series of successive stages that parallel change processes. In this early stage, you will explain to people what they can realistically expect and how things will proceed:

> My job is to act as your consultant and collaborator to help you sort out what is going on, what led to these problems, and what you can do differently in the future to produce more satisfactory results. Even though you are here for this one specific issue that is disturbing you, you will learn a process that you can apply again and again to other problems that come up in your life.

Enter the Person's World

To help someone, you have to know what is going on. This doesn't just involve whatever led the person to seek help at this time, but also the context of the problem in his or her life. The beginnings of your relationship are thus focused on learning as much as you can about the person in the shortest period of time. Basically, you are saying, "Help me to know you. What is it that you think I need to know to help you?"

Don't Ask Too Many Questions

There is a tendency to try and find out the information you need by asking questions—lots of questions—one after another: "So, what do you do with your time? Do you spend much time alone? Do you have many friends? Have you had this problem before?" These are called "close-ended" questions, meaning that they require one-word answers and tend to cut off much communication. They put you in charge, functioning like an interrogator who is empowered to direct the conversation. If, instead, you want a more equal, natural, easygoing encounter, then you will need to find other ways to keep things going. These skills will be discussed in the next chapter. For now, remind yourself not to ask questions if you can figure out another way to elicit information. When you do ask questions, do so in a way that opens rather than closes communication. For example, instead of asking "Do you have a hobby?," which could be answered (especially by a reluctant individual) with a simple yes, followed by silence waiting for your next question, you could ask instead, "What do you like to do with your free time?"

Reflect Back What You Understand

At various intervals throughout the discussion, you will attempt to build trust and understanding by letting the other person know that you are tracking accurately and perceptively what is being expressed. You will do this primarily through reflective responses (to be discussed in the next chapter) in which you communicate what you heard. These will include reflecting the content of what is said ("You hope that our time together will help you sort out this problem in a way that you can do something about it") and also the underlying feeling ("You are feeling discouraged about what has happened and pessimistic that there is anything I can do to help"). In addition to these responses inserted throughout your discussion, you will also use summary statements during regular intervals to let the person know what has been covered so far.

This is what reflective listening looks and sounds like during a few-minute interaction with a student who is first learning helping skills:

Student: "I can't get this stuff. I don't know. It just seems so . . . so . . . "

Helper: "It seems like too much for you and you're wondering if you'll ever be able to learn these skills."

Student: "Well, yeah. I mean, I look at the others and they don't seem to be having as hard of a time as I am. And you make it look so easy."

Helper: "You are making comparisons between yourself and others, concluding that you don't measure up. Furthermore, you are having some serious concerns about whether this might even be the right field for you."

Student: "Well, I always thought this was what I wanted to do. I don't really know what else I'd rather do instead. It's just that . . . it's kinda like . . . " (sighs in exasperation).

Helper: "So, you know this is what you want to do. You're just finding it so much harder than you ever imagined to learn the things you need to know. This isn't coming easily for you at all."

It's clear from this interaction that the helper tried mostly to listen and reflect back the content and feeling of what was expressed. Just as important is what wasn't done: There were no questions asked. There was no attempt to reassure the student with platitudes like "I'm sure you'll do better with practice" or "Stop comparing yourself to others." During this building stage of the relationship, what you are trying to do is create a strong connection with the other person. There will be plenty of time a little later to move toward fixing the problem, if, in fact, that is what needs to be done.

Don't Try to Do Too Much

One of the mistakes made most often by beginners is trying to do too much too soon. Even though it may sometimes feel like it, your job is *not* to fix the problem. You are not a magician or even a problem solver. Instead, your role is to create the kind of relationship that makes it safe for the person you are helping to figure out what's really going on, and then with your assistance, to come up with his or her own solution. Because so often there isn't a single resolution that's even possible, that makes it even more important for you to concentrate on just helping the person to feel respected, cherished, supported, and understood.

Work Collaboratively

For helping relationships to work well, all parties have to be invested and willing to commit themselves to a partnership. It is not in your power or control to create a good relationship unless the person you are helping feels a degree of mutual trust and respect. From the very beginning of your first interactions, you will want to make it clear that the client does most of the work. If things are not proceeding according to expectations and preferences, then he or she must take responsibility for letting you know so that adjustments can be made.

Find Out How You Are Doing

You are going to make lots of mistakes. Much of the time, you won't even be sure if you're helping someone. All too often, people never come back after a first encounter and you will never learn why: Maybe you helped them so much they didn't need any more assistance, or perhaps you did something that drove the person away. If you have been successful in creating a solid relationship, then it's safe to find out how things are going. At least once, if not more often, in every meeting, you want to ask the person how things are going, how he or she likes what is happening, and what, if anything, he or she would like to change about the direction you have been going together. This feedback is essential to select the most effective interventions that will produce the best outcomes. You will, therefore, want to spend the last few minutes of an encounter reviewing what was covered and what things were most helpful. I like to ask clients, just before they leave, "What will you think about when you leave here? What part of our talk will haunt you the most? And what do you resolve to do based on what we talked about?"

Get a Commitment to Continue

It's rare (but not impossible) that you can help someone in a single session. Most often, you will need some sort of ongoing contact to offer continued support, monitor progress, refine strategies, and generalize what was worked on to other areas of life. For this reason, you must do what you can to get people to schedule another time to get together with you. This commitment takes two different forms. First, you want the person to declare some degree of responsibility for the sessions. Second, you want to help the person translate what was discussed into some specific plan that can be worked on between sessions. After all, most of the work takes place not during the talks, but between them when people apply what they learned.

For Review

- Helping relationships are the glue that hold everything else together, especially when they are structured in such a way as to be safe, consistent, and dependable.
- Once established, the helping relationship can be used as leverage to offer support, provide honest feedback, and encourage constructive risk taking.
- Helping relationships are different from other interactions in that they are designed solely to benefit the client's needs.

For Reflection and Practice

1. Reflect on the most powerful healing relationships you have ever experienced. What made the greatest difference?

2. In a small group or with a trusted partner, talk about some of the most frequent conflicts you have experienced in your life. What have you done, most characteristically, to make matters worse?

3. Interview several people with whom you share the greatest intimacy. Ask them what about you they most appreciate.

4. Ask the same individuals (or others) what you do to push people away.

For Further Reading

Brammer, L. M., & MacDonald, G. (2007). *The helping relationship* (9th ed.). Boston: Allyn & Bacon.

Bugental, J. F. T. (1990). *Intimate journeys.* San Francisco: Jossey-Bass.

Cochran, J. L., & Cochran, N. H. (2005). *The heart of counseling: A guide to developing therapeutic relationships.* Belmont, CA: Wadsworth.

Cowan, E. W. (2005). *Ariadne's thread: Case studies in the therapeutic relationship.* Boston: Lahaska Press.

DeSole, L. M. (2006). *Making contact: The therapist's guide to conducting a successful first interview.* Boston: Pearson.

France, K., Weikel, K., & Kish, M. (2006). *Helping relationships for human service workers: Building relationships and encouraging productive change.* Springfield, IL: C. C. Thomas.

Gilbert, P., & Leahy, R. L. (2007). *The therapeutic relationship in cognitive behavioral psychotherapies.* New York: Routledge.

Hubble, M. A., Duncan, B. C., & Miller, S. D. (Eds.). (1999). *The heart and soul of change: What works in therapy.* Washington, DC: American Psychological Association.

Moore, T. (1994). *Soul mates: Honoring the mysteries of love and relationship.* New York: HarperCollins.

Norcross, J. C. (2002). *Psychotherapy relationships that work.* New York: Oxford University Press.

Rogers, C. R. (1980). *A way of being.* Boston: Houghton Mifflin.

Yalom, I. (1989). *Love's executioner and other tales of psychotherapy.* New York: Basic Books.

5

Exploration Skills

Although you may feel anxious—and impatient—to get going and help
someone already, you will want to explore thoroughly what the situation is all about before you attempt some intervention. Nothing can be more
dangerous than jumping in to try to fix things when you only know a fraction of what is going on. Perhaps the problem that you are seeing is symptomatic of other difficulties beyond your awareness. There could be some
undiagnosed physical malady. Maybe the complaint that has been brought
to your attention isn't the most pressing problem at all. It could be a test. It
could be a smokescreen. It could be a distraction, or even a cry for attention.
There is often no way to tell until you conduct a thorough assessment and
exploration.

If you were feeling pain in your abdominal region and consulted a physician for help, you would hardly want her to conduct a cursory exam and
then assume it's the stomach flu that she has seen a lot of lately. It might very
well be that, but it could also be a lot of other things, from indigestion or a
muscle strain to appendicitis or cancer. You'd want her to get some background on you, to get to know you first. You would want her to conduct a
complete examination and order all reasonable tests. You might feel more
comfortable with some intrusive procedure if you were certain that she had
made an accurate diagnosis and knew what she was doing.

This same process holds true with the helping process as well. During the
exploration phase, you are collecting all relevant information you can in the
quickest period of time. This will help you with your diagnosis and treatment planning. Far more than that, however, you are using exploration skills

to help the person do the work. You want to act as a mirror as best you can, to reflect back clearly and without distortion what you hear, see, observe, sense, and feel. If you have done your job well, then the individual (or family) can put together the pieces of the puzzle based on some new understanding of their lives.

Internal Attitudes

Helping begins with what you do inside your own head and heart. There are certain attitudes you want to adopt when you are working that are in marked contrast to those when you are operating in your "civilian" life. Whereas you might feel judgmental and critical of people when you are walking around in your world, such attitudes are not constructive during your helping role. Furthermore, despite your best efforts to hide these critical judgments, others can also be exquisitely sensitive to your inner states. They can tell when they are being judged harshly. They can feel your disdain. One of the disadvantages of a true empathic connection is that others often know what you are thinking, just like you can at times read their minds. It is for this reason that you don't want to pretend certain internal attitudes; you want to really feel them.

In addition to putting yourself in a place where you suspend criticism and prejudices, you also want to adopt an internal state such that you are feeling clear headed and poised. I encourage beginning helpers to begin each session with a cleansing breath, just like in yoga or meditation, in which you close your eyes for a moment, take a deep breath, and gently push aside all distractions so you can give your full attention to this other person you want to help. Any time you feel intruding thoughts, distracting ideas, or critical judgments, you just gently push them aside.

You might try this right now. Close your eyes for a minute. Take a deep breath from the center of your abdomen, cleansing your body and clearing your mind as you exhale. When you open your eyes, center your concentration and focus your energy on a single point. This is exactly what you would do before you begin a helping conversation to remain centered.

You want to make yourself into a perfect receptacle, that is, to tune yourself to the point where you can hear, see, and feel things that ordinarily are beyond awareness. You want to be in an ideal state of mind to take in whatever is put out by the other person. This is what will allow you to pick up on things that are beneath the surface.

Your internal attitudes should not only include monitoring the parts of you that lean toward being critical and judgmental, but also communicating positive messages of warmth, caring, respect, and genuineness. All helping is predicated on trust: If the client does not see you as accessible and understanding, then he or she is unlikely to open up.

Attending Behaviors

If on the inside you are concentrating with all your energy on remaining clear, then on the outside you want to do everything in your power to communicate total interest. These attending behaviors involve several distinct aspects that are summarized in Table 5.1.

Table 5.1   Attending Checklist

- ☑ Face the person fully.
- ☑ Communicate intense interest.
- ☑ Give undivided attention.
- ☑ Maintain natural eye contact.
- ☑ Be sensitive to cultural preferences.
- ☑ Make your face expressive.
- ☑ Nod your head. A lot.
- ☑ Present yourself authentically.

1. *Body position.* Remove any obstacles (like a desk) between you and the other person. Adjust the space between you so it is a comfortable distance. Face the person fully. Lean forward, but not to the point where you intrude in the other person's space. Communicate with your whole being that you are riveted by what the other person has to say. Give your complete and undivided attention. You will be surprised how much this alone can be healing for others because it's so rare that any of us is accustomed to being really listened to.

2. *Eye contact.* Keep things natural, but use your eyes to make deep contact. If there is more than one person present, then use your eyes to draw each person in. Be sensitive to individual and cultural differences because some people feel invaded rather than soothed by intense scrutiny.

3. *Facial expressions.* The person is watching you carefully to see how you are responding to what is being said. Are you understanding what is going on? Because most people are not used to being listened to very well, you are being scrutinized, skeptically, to see if you are really paying attention, and if so, whether you hear what is really being expressed. You can use your facial

expressions not only to show that you are listening intently, but also to resonate with what the person is feeling and expressing. You can use words to say that you understand, or you can use your face to communicate the same thing.

4. *Nonverbal gestures.* One other way to let the person know that you are tracking the conversation is to use other attending behaviors, such as nodding your head and gesturing with your hands. The key with all these attending behaviors is to use everything in your power to communicate your total and complete concentration on the interaction. Prove that you are listening by showing your interest with your behavior.

Practice Makes Perfect

Contrary to what you might think, attending and other helping behaviors are not at all natural. If they were, then everyone would demonstrate the kind of focused devotion that is unique to helping relationships. In truth, people get used to having the divided interest of others. Take a single day in your life and keep close track of how other people respond to you. Notice the number of multiple tasks that they carry on at the same time they are supposedly listening to you. Watch people's faces when they listen to you, even those who love you the most, and notice how their attention wanders and their interests shift. Monitor how often people speak to you at the same time they are doing other things—waving at someone else, opening mail, shifting papers, grooming themselves, answering the phone, or otherwise showing that although they might be interested in what you have to say, it's not so important that they are willing to put everything else on hold.

In addition to any time you spend in class practicing attending behaviors, you will want to find as many opportunities as you can to apply these skills to your life. After all, these behaviors, which are so useful in professional encounters, are just as powerful when employed with those you care about the most. Next time you are engaged in conversation with a friend, family member, or coworker, make a commitment to put aside all other distractions so you can give the person your full attention. Use your eyes, facial expressions, and nonverbal gestures to communicate you are tracking what is said. Try to make it habitual when you train yourself to practice proper attending behaviors.

Presenting Yourself

So far, we have been dealing with rather concrete behaviors that are crucial in helping relationships. Although I don't wish to diminish in any way the importance of attending and other specific behavior during the exploration phase of helping, the way you present yourself to others involves something more than how you act.

At the same time that you are studying your clients and trying to figure out what is going on, what they really want from you, and what you should do to be most helpful, they are checking you out as well. They are trying to decide how much to tell you. They are wondering if they are doing the right thing by consulting you; maybe it would be better to just handle things on their own.

You will wish to give considerable attention to the ways you present yourself to others. As stated by one popular advertising slogan, "Image is everything!" You will want to follow that advice, at least to the extent that you look the part of a confident expert.

Dress yourself as you would for a performance in a play, thinking through how you want to be perceived by others. You will want to look professional, but also relaxed. If you are working mostly with kids, you'd dress down a bit. If, on the other hand, you are working with people in the business world, you would similarly dress appropriately for that population.

In addition to your wardrobe, you will also wish to present yourself in a manner consistent with what your clients expect looks like an expert. To meet this image, which varies considerably among different cultures, regions, professions, and age groups, you will want to do some research among your peers. Although in later stages, once you have developed a solid relationship, images and appearances mean much less, initially this presentation is very important.

Listening

Now that you look and act the part, or at least pretend to know what you are doing, you will need to do considerably more than attend to what the person is saying. The single most important skill in helping someone is listening (see Table 5.2 for a checklist of points to remember). I'll stay that again: *Listening is the most crucial helping skill.*

I am not talking here about the kind of listening you usually do, in which you half-heartedly pay attention, nor am I referring to merely attending to what is being said. Real listening, *deep* listening, involves such complete concentration that you can't do anything else at the same time. You are focusing not just on the words that are being said aloud, but also on what is going on beneath the surface. Taking into account the context of the situation, the background and culture of your client, the nonverbal cues that are presented,

Table 5.2   Listening Checklist

☑ Clear your mind.

☑ Empathize: Crawl inside the other's skin.

☑ Concentrate completely.

☑ Watch carefully for nonverbal cues.

☑ Don't just listen, but really hear.

☑ Ask yourself what the person is really saying.

☑ Identify underlying feelings, as well as surface content.

☑ Use your heart, as well as your head, to divine meaning.

and any other information at your disposal, what are you sensing is really being expressed at this moment?

Someone says to you, for example, "So, to tell you the truth, I don't really care that much about her one way or the other." He is talking about the relationship with his girlfriend that just ended.

What did you hear this person just say?

You can't answer that question, of course, because you don't have access to enough information. You don't have any visual cues to tell you what he really meant by this situation. You couldn't hear the tone of voice. You don't know the history of the situation. But if you were sitting in the room with this person, if you had spent time with him before, if you could see him and hear his voice, then you would be asking yourself these questions: What is the guy really saying at this moment? What does he mean by this? He is saying he doesn't care that the relationship ended, even prefacing that statement with the claim that this is the truth (as if he knows that sounds improbable), but I sense that he does care quite a lot. Furthermore, he seems so wounded by this break-up he is reluctant to even talk about it now.

Of course, while all this processing is going on, the man has already moved on to something else. Obviously, then, you don't have a lot of time to decode the underlying meaning to statements, or else you'll never get the chance to formulate a response, much less say it aloud. Nevertheless, while you are in your "helping stance," you are listening with what has become called your "third ear." You are not only hearing the words that were said, but you are listening with your inner being, attending not only to the surface statement, but also its underlying meanings.

Time to Practice

Even with limited cues, you can still deduce something about the possible message that is being communicated—if you listen carefully.

Monica is 7 years old and has been playing quietly with her brother, that is, until he ripped a toy out of her hands and bolted out of the room. Monica runs up to you in a panic, her lip quivering, tears pooling in her eyes. You ask her what's wrong, and she mumbles, half to herself: "Nothing."

Now, what do you sense she is really communicating by that remark? Does she actually mean to say that nothing is wrong?

If you surmised that she is feeling hurt and angry, you are probably in the vicinity of what is going on. If you further deduce that she is also embarrassed by her situation and feels reluctant to talk about it, then you have probably also hit the mark. I use words like "probably" because you can't really know what is happening; you can only form hypotheses that will have to be tested when you choose to respond. For now, however, in the second or two you have before you say something appropriate, you first ask yourself, "What is Monica saying to me right now?"

Whatever answer you get will suggest a particular response or intervention. If you hear that nothing is really going on, then you might respond in one way. If you hear anger as the primary message, you will say something else. If you hear hurt or sadness, then you might react differently again. In each case, you are listening not only with your two ears, but with your intuition, your "felt sense" about what she is saying.

Knowing what you now understand about surface and deep communications, walk around attending to the underlying meanings behind what people say to you and others every day. Sensitize yourself, as much as you can, to listen with your third ear. When you are in the mood, ask yourself what a person is really communicating with a particular gesture, expression, or message. Become aware, as much as you can, of the hidden, disguised, and unrecognized portions of what is said in everyday conversations.

Eliciting Information

Your main task during exploration is to find out what is going on with the person you are helping. At the very least, you want to know what the person sees as the main problem. You also wish to learn a host of other things that would be helpful in formulating a diagnosis and treatment plan.

Although it might appear as if asking questions would be the most logical, direct way to find out the information you need, there are also other,
more subtle ways to get a person to provide you with valuable data. As
I mentioned before, side effects of asking too many questions are that you
appear as an interrogator, as well as make the person dependent on you to
keep things going. Note in the following conversation how stilted and one-
sided the interaction seems:

Helper: "What can I help you with today?"

Client: [Shrugs] "I'm not really sure."

Helper: "You're not sure?"

Client: "No."

Helper: "Is this the first time you've asked for help about this problem?"

Client: "Uh-huh."

Helper: "So you don't know where to start?"

Client: "Right."

Helper: "When did you first become aware that you were having difficulty?"

There is nothing actually wrong with the agenda the helper is following.
She is trying to uncover what the client is struggling with, a not-unreasonable
place to begin. The client, who appears reticent, or at least shy, is not being
the most cooperative participant in this process. Yet a pattern is already being
established in which the helper is the one who is asking the questions, which
are eliciting one-word answers. This type of close-ended question doesn't work
very effectively to find out much information. Moreover, it leads to a type of
relationship that may not be what you want to create.

In the next section, we will cover ways to ask questions when you can't
get data in other ways. It is usually preferable to use probes and other leading skills that don't rely on a direct interrogative style.

Note in the following excerpt how the helper attempts to gather information in ways other than asking questions:

Helper: "I understand you've been having difficulty with something."

Client: [Shrugs] "I'm not really sure."

Helper: "It's difficult to put things into words." [The helper reflects back
        what she thinks the client is really saying.]

Client: "Yeah. You could say that."

Helper: [Waits patiently, maintaining interest and attending behaviors, but communicating clearly that whatever happens next is up to the client.]

Client: [Sighs] "I suppose I should start at the beginning."

Helper: "That might be helpful." [Hangs back, even after the initial tease. Continues waiting while the client formulates his thoughts.]

Client: "Well, it's just . . . I don't know . . ."

Helper: "Go on." [Offers a supportive prompt]

Make no mistake: The helper is dying to ask about a hundred questions. She is feeling impatient inside, but checks those feelings as much as she can. She knows she has to go at the client's pace, and he is obviously having a hard time. She can always revert to asking questions at a later time; for now, she is trying to be as encouraging as she can, to let the client set the pace. If this laborious, awkward conversation continues much longer, then she will probably have to switch gears and try something else.

Asking Questions

As should be clear from the preceding section, asking questions is a mixed blessing. It does get you the information you want in the most direct fashion, but often at a price. One guideline: Ask questions when you can't think of another way to get the information you need.

When you do rely on questions to elicit background, try to mix them up with other skills that will be covered later. Otherwise, you will set up a predictable pattern whereby you maintain complete control of and responsibility for the interview.

In many cases, much of the information you need will already be available on intake forms and other questionnaires that may have been completed. If so, you can easily refer to that data to probe more deeply, as in, "I noticed on this form you filled out that you have four siblings, three sisters and one brother. Tell me more about your relationships with various family members."

Even this wasn't framed as a direct question, but as a request. When you do ask it in a question form, make sure you do so in a way that is open ended rather than close ended. Compare, for example, the two different ways the question may be framed:

Closed: "Are you close to your siblings?"

This could get you the information you need, but just as likely (especially with a reluctant client), you could hear a one-word response of yes or no.

Open: "What are your relationships like with your siblings?"

In this case, it is still possible to give an evasive response, but it would be a lot harder to do so.

There is one clear, definitive piece of advice on this subject. In fact, if there is one single thing you could do to improve your competence as helper, besides becoming a better listener, it would be to learn open-ended questioning. Even most professional interviewers on television and in law enforcement don't seem to understand this basic concept. If you don't believe me, pay attention to the next talk-show host and listen to the rapid-fire questions, one after another: "Do you like living in Hollywood?" "Are you going to remain there now that you will be shooting your next film in England?" "Would you say that this next film will be the capstone of your career?" The only reason why you don't notice that the interviewer is so poorly skilled is because his or her subject is so eager to promote a film. You will not be so fortunate.

When you ask questions, you should not only plan them in such a way that they open communication, but also so that they elicit the most information possible. Well-formed questions will get you lots of stuff that you never intended to explore in the first place. For example, you could ask, "Where would you like to go from here?" In this instance, you intended to find out when and if the person would like to talk again another time. Instead, the client interpreted it another way, and began telling you about future goals. In other words, how the person interprets your question can be as invaluable as the actual answer.

The best questions are those that elicit responses that are especially revealing. Some favorites are similar to the following:

- What would a typical day in your life be like? Describe what you do from the moment you wake up to the moment you fall asleep.
- What have you done in your life that you are most proud of? What about most ashamed of?
- When was the last time that you felt really in control in your life? How was that different from now?
- Who are you closest to in the world?
- What are a few things that nobody in the world knows about you that would be especially helpful for me to know?
- How is this present problem you are having familiar to you? How have you experienced something similar in the past?
- What is an area that you feel especially resistant to getting into?
- When you leave here today, what is the one thing that will haunt you the most?

This is just a meager sampling of possible areas of exploration. With questions, you are trying to supplement the exploration you have undertaken by other means. You don't wish to appear as an interrogator, but you do need to gather more detailed information to proceed further.

As with all the other skills presented, you must find opportunities to apply what you are learning in your personal life. Because we are talking about upgrading and changing your whole communication style, I will remind you again that most of these skills can be used in every facet of your relationships, not just with those you are trying to help. Try to catch yourself asking close-ended questions ("Did you have a good time?" or "Do you want to go to a movie or a play?") and instead rephrase them in an open-ended way ("What happened last night?" or "What would you like to do this evening?"). These skills take lots of practice because you must break long-standing habits that often get in the way.

Assessing Strengths and Resources

Ordinarily, when you might think of assessment and diagnosis, you would associate this process with identifying problems, uncovering maladaptive behaviors, and classifying symptoms of mental disorder. Even clients hold this assumption when they come in expecting to talk about what is most going wrong in their lives.

Although it is certainly critical during the exploration phase of helping to assess problem areas and formulate tentative diagnoses that might suggest certain treatment strategies, it is also extremely important to help people articulate what is going right in their lives, as well as what might be wrong. This includes identifying the internal resources, evidence of resilience, and social supports that will be most useful during the helping process.

This task of taking inventory of strengths, as well as weaknesses, is more challenging than you might imagine. Many people believe that when they seek the services of a helper, it is to complain about everything that is not working; they are often surprised when they are pressed to look for exceptions. Yet this movement, called "positive psychology," encourages people to focus on the resources and strengths at their disposal. Note how this unfolds in the following dialogue with someone who has been experiencing chronic and debilitating symptoms associated with multiple sclerosis, a serious, progressive neurological disorder:

Client: "So I feel this numbness on the left side of my face, right here [points to cheek and chin]. I can't feel anything. I can't even tell if I'm smiling or frowning."

Helper: "That's another thing that you can't control, making you feel even more helpless and powerless." [Reflecting client's feelings]

Client: "Yeah, but it's more than that. The doctor told me I might have to have another operation for a bladder infection. And then there's . . ."

Helper: "I know there are so many difficult challenges you are facing, so many symptoms that are uncomfortable and painful and frustrating. [Validating experience] You've talked at length today about all the things that have been going wrong lately—with your body and your life. I'm wondering, though, what has been going well?" [Focusing on the positive]

Client: "What do you mean?"

Helper: "Among all the difficulties you are dealing with lately, what is something that seems to be going reasonably well for you?"

What the helper is asking the client to do is somewhat difficult. Resistance and confusion is to be expected. The client is used to talking about what is wrong, and the helper is trying to balance this by talking about other aspects of life that may not be a problem right now or may even be going quite well. For instance, in this case, even with the physical problems, the client is enjoying closer intimacy with her family. Although it is difficult for her to take time off work, she has also been enjoying having discretionary time to read novels and watch movies.

When doing an assessment and exploration of client issues, it is important to examine positive as well as negative aspects of the client's life and experience. This investigation can often be empowering in and of itself because it helps the person look at problems in a larger, more complete context. This kind of investigation also plants greater hope and positive expectations for the future.

In a later chapter examining action-oriented skills, one common intervention is the use of homework and accountability to check on client progress. Yet again, there should be an emphasis on things that are going well in addition to those that are not. One application of the positive psychology movement that is useful in this regard simply asks clients to note (or better yet, to write down) three good things that happened that day and what they believed led to this result. Even for people who are depressed, such a positive focus helps them to find greater balance between perceived misfortunes and blessings.

Formulating Diagnoses

Even if the nature of your job does not involve the use of the *DSM* (the *Diagnostic and Statistical Manual of Mental Disorders* by the American Psychiatric Association, which is used as the standard reference source), you will still need to think diagnostically before you attempt any intervention. After all, how can you possibly do anything to be helpful if you don't have a clear notion (or even a general idea) about what you want to do?

Imagine, for example, that someone consults you because he or she is feeling depressed. How will your proceed with this case?

I hope your immediate response is, Well, that depends on what's going on. What kind of depression are we dealing with here? What does it mean in this person's life, at this particular time?

Depression, and all other forms of emotional disturbance, are tricky entities about which we still don't understand as much as we would like. What we do know thus far is that "depression" or "anxiety" are not single conditions that suggest consistent interventions. Someone who describes himself as anxious could actually be diagnosed with situational stress that results from a single crisis in his life. He may also be showing signs of generalized anxiety that have been relatively stable, chronic symptoms. Or perhaps he is experiencing panic attacks or a phobic disorder, or even post-traumatic stress. Each type of anxiety would involve a different treatment strategy.

Likewise with the case of our depressed person: During your exploration efforts, you must make an accurate diagnosis of what kind of depression is being experienced. Is this characteristic of "dysthymia," a sort of chronic, low-grade depressed mood? In this instance, you would plan a relatively long-term relationship to get at underlying thinking patterns and lifestyle issues.

Perhaps we are dealing instead with something more severe, such as bipolar disorder (also known as manic-depression) or "endogenous" depression, both of which are caused by biochemical imbalances. In both cases, the depression is not so much elicited by stressors in the environment as they are by one's hormonal, endocrine, and neurological systems. In each case, there are biologically based symptoms of sleep disruption, change in eating patterns, and so on. Both of these kinds of depression are usually treated by some form of medication with counseling.

When the kind of depression (or any problem) is clearly the result of some particular adjustment to a developmental transition (leaving home, getting married, birth of a child) or life crisis (divorce, financial problem, grief issue), then some form of counseling is especially helpful. If you can make the determination that some adjustment reaction is going on, that the condition is acute, and that you can rule out any organic problem or underlying personality disorder, then the prognosis for counseling is excellent.

I mentioned the issue of personality in passing, but it is actually quite an important variable. In addition to whatever psychological symptoms a person is presenting, there are two other important areas that you will wish to check out. Both of them are covered in any standardized psychiatric or psychological assessment. Whether you will have access to standardized psychological tests or the results of a formal intake interview that includes a *DSM* diagnosis, you will still need to explore areas related to organic and personality functioning.

Counseling deals mostly with psychological health, although physical functioning also plays a major role. Be sure to find out about a person's medical history, whether he or she is experiencing any physical complaints in addition to psychological ones, or whether stated problems could even be caused by underlying, undiagnosed illnesses such as tumors, neurological disease, or other maladies. This is one reason why it is important to consult regularly with medically trained personnel who can rule out such organic factors.

Another sticky issue has to do with a client's underlying personality style, which may exacerbate problems or get in the way of attempts to be helpful. In its most extreme form, some people are inclined to act in certain ways that are self-destructive, are harmful to others, or involve a characteristic style of interaction that may be described as manipulative. You probably know some people like this and know how challenging they are to be around. Imagine, therefore, how difficult it can be to try to help folks like them when it involves getting them to be revealing and honest.

Whether the dysfunctional personality style qualifies as a full-fledged disorder or not (usually meeting certain criteria), you will want take into account characteristic interaction patterns that can undermine your treatment efforts. A brief summary of the personality styles that are most commonly diagnosed include the following:

- *Borderline personality.* Someone who exhibits self-destructive behavior and shows a pattern of unstable relationships.
- *Narcissistic personality.* Someone who is extremely self-centered with an exaggerated sense of self-importance.
- *Sociopathic personality.* Someone who is exploitive in relationships with no remorse.
- *Schizoid personality.* Someone who is odd, eccentric, and detached from relationships.
- *Paranoid personality.* Someone who is extremely suspicious and fearful that others are planning harm.

Putting this all together, your diagnostic efforts should be focused on assessing a client's characteristic functioning, relevant background data, medical history, presenting symptoms, social-cultural factors, and personality style. Following a model suggested by the *DSM*, you would also want to check the person's highest level of functioning in the past year and compare that with current levels.

Assessing Risk

One exception to asking close-ended questions is when you are assessing whether someone is at risk to hurt themselves or someone else. If you suspect that someone you are seeing is a suicidal risk or a danger to act out in some way (physical abuse, sexual abuse, violence, etc.), then you *must* determine whether some immediate intervention is indicated.

With respect to suicidal risk, you would need to ask the following questions, in some cases, framed in a close-ended way to get definitive responses:

- *Are you thinking of harming yourself in some way?* Contrary to popular belief, you don't put this idea in someone's head. You must get a clear answer to this question or assume the worst.
- *Is there someone else in your family, or someone else you've been close to, who has ever tried to kill himself or herself?* Is there a precedent for showing the client that suicide is a legitimate escape to a problem? You want to find out if this behavior has been modeled before.
- *Do you have a plan for how you might kill yourself?* The risk of suicide is much greater if someone has a specific idea of what they would do ("Yes, I have access to a gun that I know is in a box in the attic.") versus someone who hasn't thought it through ("I don't know exactly. Maybe take some pills or something.").
- *Do you have the background that is most associated with suicidal acts?* Those who are most likely to act on their impulses are those who have what is called an "agitated" depression, meaning that they are very disturbed but also have the energy to carry through on their despair and hopelessness. They tend to be older adults (older than 60). They live alone. They are divorced, separated, or widowed. They are unemployed.
- *Is there excessive use of alcohol or drugs?* As you would imagine, mind-altering substances impair judgment, dull inhibitions, and lead to self-destructive behavior.
- *Have you taken steps to close your affairs?* Is there evidence that the person has already begun the process of self-destruction? Common examples are those when people have started to put their affairs in order (drafted a will, cleaned the house, written a note, planned their funeral).

- *Have you attempted suicide previously?* Those who are at greatest risk have made attempts before. Find out whether these actions were genuine suicidal acts or gestures to secure attention.

Keep in mind that predicting suicidal or homicidal behavior is a very risky proposition in and of itself. Even the most experienced clinicians, with access to the most complete records and assessment instruments, still can't forecast whether someone might act impulsively. So although the previous guidelines are good general indicators, you must not be too confident that you can tell what might happen. When in doubt, seek consultation with a supervisor. Better yet, any time there is a suicidal risk, get supervision or at least a consultation with someone else.

Responding to Content

Finally we are at the point where you actually need to do some counseling. That's not to say that the assessment process can't be therapeutic in and of itself, because many people do find it helpful to review their lives in a systematic way. It puts things in perspective. It gets them thinking analytically about recurrent patterns. In fact, quite a few times, you will find that a single exploratory interview will be enough to spark significant changes, especially if you don't underestimate the power of what can be done from a single session.

The most frequent skill used by helpers, in conjunction with the next one related to responding to feelings, is called *paraphrasing*. In its simplest form, you take what you have heard (remember, you have been listening *very* carefully to surface and deep meanings) and respond with a reflection on the essential content that has been expressed.

Generally, when first learning this skill, you might try "parroting" first, although you would almost never do this in a real session. It is kind of like "training wheels" for those learning to ride a bike, in that it provides you with an intermediate step before you try things on your own.

In parroting, you repeat verbatim exactly what you heard the other person say. While this might sound silly, it is actually a technique sometimes used in marriage counseling with partners who don't listen to one another. Each partner is instructed to repeat, to the other person's satisfaction, exactly what was just said before he or she is allowed to respond. That way each can be certain he or she was heard, a problem that often gets in the way of communication. Parroting looks and sounds something like this:

Client: "I just can't seem to get on top of things."

Helper: "You can't get on top of things."

Client: "That's what I just said."

Helper: "That what you just said."

Client: "If you don't stop repeating what I said, I'm going to hit you."

Helper: "If you don't stop . . ." [Slap]

Well, you get the idea. Obviously, you wouldn't actually use parroting unless you panicked and couldn't think of anything else to say (usually people are so preoccupied with what they're saying, they don't notice you anyway). It does, however, train you to practice listening to what is being said and then prove you heard by repeating it back.

In theory, when you use rephrasing, you are acting like a kind of mirror, reflecting back both the content and the feeling (the next skill to be covered) of what you heard. This leads people to clarify their thoughts and feelings, as well as gets them talking more about what is going on in their life, their minds (in the case of content), and their hearts (in the case of feelings).

When paraphrasing, you are concentrating on the essence of what a person just said, at least as far as the content, and then reflecting that back.

A client says to you, for example, "I can't seem to get motivated much any more. My parents are getting old and they can't help out much. My health isn't what it used to be either."

How might you rephrase that statement? (Do it in your head.)

Hopefully, your response sounded something like this: "You're having problems with your health and getting going on things that are important to you. You aren't getting much help from others you depend on either."

Notice in this paraphrase that the focus remained on the content of what was expressed, rather than the feeling. There are reasons for this choice. Perhaps it is too early in the session to get into threatening material. Maybe things are happening so quickly that you don't have time to reflect feelings that are deeper, or you could be stalling for time until you can think of something more profound to say. In any event, you are keeping the exploration going. You have proven that you understood what was said. And you have encouraged the client to look more deeply.

The steps involved in paraphrasing involve asking yourself the following questions internally:

1. What did I just hear?

2. What is the essence of the content just expressed?

3. How can I rephrase this in a way that is both concise and captures the spirit of what was said?

A few cautions when using paraphrases, as well as other skills. If you wait until a pause, you might never get a chance to say anything at all. At times, you will have to insert your comments, even interrupt, to keep the conversation focused when someone is rambling:

Client: "It's just so hard on all of us, what with little money and all. And things are just getting worse. The other day I was in town and I was talking to Simon. You know Simon? He's the guy who . . ."

Helper: "So things have been getting worse for you day by day. You have less money and yet more things you have to do."

Client: "Well, yeah, that's true. I was thinking maybe I should get another part-time job, but if I do that they'll be nobody around to take care of things around home. There's just so many chores to do. I've got to repaint the barn. Then there's all them animals to take care of. I wonder if . . ."

Helper: "You were saying that maybe another job might bring in more money, but then you were considering the disadvantages, too. When it comes right down to it, you've got more choices then you thought at first, even if each one might not be ideal."

Client: "I guess you're right. That's what I did say, didn't I?"

There are some limits to this sort of skill, in that it stays pretty much on a content level, keeping people in their heads. That's why there are other things you can do to in addition that can take people to a deeper level. Nevertheless, rephrasing is the "bread and butter" of what helpers do. It's relatively harmless. It buys you time until you can do or say something else. It lets the person know you are tracking the conversation accurately, and it furthers the exploration process.

Responding to Feelings

Reflecting someone's feelings is one of the easiest skills to learn and yet is probably the most difficult to master. Like paraphrasing, you can learn the mechanics in just a few minutes, even though you will probably need a lifetime to develop the sensitivity, intuition, and deftness needed to really help people to explore on the deepest level.

What you are trying to do with this skill is move people beyond the content of their statements to look more closely at the underlying feelings that are being expressed. There are many good reasons why you might want to do this. For one, people might be denying or unaware of how they are feeling. Second, emotional arousal and resolution is one of the keys to promoting lasting change. In a sense, what you are doing is alternating both reflections of content and feeling to help people clarify (a) what they are saying, (b) what they might be experiencing beneath the surface, and (c) what feelings are most present, and therefore, most influential.

In the following interaction, notice how the helper very quickly moves the client from a rather superficial conversation to something much deeper:

Client: "I was telling you before about all these medical problems I've been having lately. First, it's this dizziness. Then I can't seem to eat anything lately . . ."

Helper: "It must be so frightening not to know what's going to happen next."

Client: "It's just such an annoyance, too. I mean, I can't seem to plan anything. I don't know when I'll feel up to it. The other day I was just so sick."

Helper: [Nods head, encouraging the client to continue.]

Client: "I've got this pain that comes and goes, you know. I just never know . . ."

Helper: "It feels like you've lost control over your own body. And if you can't count on that, what can you count on?"

Client: "Yeah. I wonder if it's even worth it to keep trying."

Helper: "Sometimes you just want to give up."

Client: "Well, what's the point? What would you do if you were in my shoes?"

Helper: "You feel so lost, as if things are utterly hopeless and you have no way out."

Notice even in this last response, the helper resists the urge to answer a direct question, which instead she treats as a statement attached to an underlying feeling. In each of her interventions, she tries to hone in on what feeling seems most present in the client's communication. Then she responds by reflecting back what she heard expressed.

This may look pretty easy, but it is actually quite difficult to break old habits. Beginners, in particular, like to ask lots of questions. Imagine, for example, someone less skilled responding with, "So, where do you feel the pain?" or "Have you had this problem long?" Another common error is to stay with content of the communication rather than going after the deeper feeling: "So, you've been having a lot of medical problems lately, more than usual."

There's nothing disastrous, or even inappropriate, about this last response; it just reinforces a superficial talk about symptoms rather than getting to what the person is feeling. Because human beings are both thinking and feeling beings, it's important to balance discussion of both sides.

When you decide to focus on the affective dimension of a person's experience, you will want to proceed as follows:

1. Attend carefully to the nonverbal and verbal cues that accompany the content of the communication.

2. Acknowledge nonverbally and verbally that you are tracking what is being said.

3. Decode the underlying meaning of the verbalization.

4. Ask yourself what feelings strike you as most present for the person in this moment.

5. Use empathy (crawling inside the other person's skin) to imagine what you would feel in this situation.

6. Formulate a response that reflects back what you have heard and sensed.

7. Continue the exploration along the same lines until you have gone to the point at which it's time to try something else.

Putting these steps into action, picture someone who is talking to you about some irritating event that just occurred. While on his way to see you, he had a close call in traffic in which someone cut him off. He seems unable to let go of the incident:

Client: "I can't believe this guy didn't even look over at me. He didn't even see me! I could have been killed! What a damn idiot! I don't know what gets into people like that. They shouldn't even be allowed to drive."

You realize at this point that you need to say something, or the guy is about to go off on a rant about something you or he can't fix anyway. Unless you say something now, you could lose the whole session while he raves and complains about the poor state of the world. It's not that this wouldn't feel good for him to let off steam, it's just that your time to be helpful is so limited that you have to keep him on track, or at least on the path that you believe is most useful.

You have no doubt that there is a lot of feeling going on for him right now, but he seems more comfortable focusing on the other guy rather than his own feelings. So, first step: What do you sense he is feeling? Forget about the content of the story, and stay with the affect.

He definitely sounds angry, but he also seems frightened. Even terrified. He just had a near-death experience, and even though he's acting like it was only a minor annoyance, you can tell that something about this episode has really gotten to him. His hands are shaking, and the intensity of his expression is way out of proportion to what actually happened.

You decide to stick with his anger first, and so you reflect that back to him: "You're infuriated that people like this guy can almost literally run right over you, as if you don't exist."

"It's the same old crap," he spits out with surprising vehemence, "that I have to face every day I go to work. People taking advantage of me. People don't care. They . . ."

Bingo. You're onto something.

Was this, therefore, the "correct" choice of feeling to focus on? There's really no way to tell for certain. One of the frustrating, confusing, annoying, overwhelming, exciting (pick one) aspects of this field is that there are so many choices you can make about what to do or say, and there's no way to know if any one of them was the best one. Of course, you can tell if what you did continues the deep-level exploration or not. At this point, though, you aren't sure whether to focus on the anger, or the fear that was stirred up, or some other area. Eventually, if you keep listening actively and if you continue to probe, to reflect back what you hear, see, sense, and feel, he will explore the areas that he most needs to at that time (see Table 5.3 for a summary of exploration skill options). Your job is to be patient, to act as a mirror of his experience, and to create an atmosphere that makes it safe for him to say out loud what he thinks and feels.

Try It Out

The best way to learn reflective listening is in small, successive steps. Find someone you can work with, either a classmate, a friend, or family member. Ask him or her to talk to you for a few minutes about anything—it doesn't have to be a big deal.

While the person is speaking to you, practice all your attending behaviors. Take a deep, cleansing breath so you can push aside all distractions, and give the person your full attention.

Table 5.3   Exploration Skills

Skill	Client Statement	Helper Response
Paraphrase	"I'm just not doing well."	"You're having a hard time."
Reflection of feeling	"It's just so tough being on my own."	"You're feeling really isolated and confused, beginning to question whether you made the right choice."
Open-ended question	"No matter what I do, I'm stuck."	"What do you imagine is the worst that can happen next?"
Summary	"I don't know. Maybe I'll give up."	"So you have some real concerns about your resilience, whether you can bounce back after so many setbacks. You also have talked about the doubt and confusion you feel."

During this conversation, you are only allowed to do three things:

1. Nod your head a lot and show the person you are listening.

2. Paraphrase at times to reflect back the content of the communication.

3. Make an effort to reflect the feelings you hear as well.

It would be best to start with a simple structure. Use the "stem" sentence, "You feel . . . ," and then fill in the blank with a feeling word. The conversation should go something like this:

Friend: "I've just got so much work to do and just no time to do it all."

You: "You feel, uh, tired."

Friend: "Well, no, I'm not so much tired as I am nervous about how I'm doing in school."

Isn't this beautiful? You can be flat-out wrong, miss the mark, and it still leads to more exploration. That's why this is such a powerful skill!

You: "You're feeling scared."

Friend: "I just don't know if I'm cut out for this sort of thing."

That was pretty superficial, but again, it doesn't matter much. You are showing you are listening just as carefully as you can. You definitely get points for trying, as your clients will forgive you for being wrong or missing the point as long as they sense you're trying.

You: "You're feeling some doubt about whether you made the right choice."

Friend: "Well, how is a person supposed to know if what they're doing is the right thing or not?"

This time, you broke from the simple structure a little, reflecting back not only the feeling you heard, but also the reason attached to it. Now you face a trap of sorts: It seems like you've just been asked a question. But you're going to still ignore the question and go after the feeling behind it. You'll also try to summarize or paraphrase what you've heard so far:

You: "You're really questioning whether you've made the right choice to do what you want. You're wondering if it might be too late to change your mind, and you're feeling scared that you might be committed to a course that really isn't right for you."

That wasn't too hard, was it? Actually it was. Go out and try these basic reflective skills with several different partners. If possible, record the brief conversations so you can review your performance afterward. Trust me: Your first efforts will not go nearly as well as you hoped. You will feel awkward and artificial. You will feel terrified of saying the wrong thing. You may panic and not know what to say. That's fine, though. What is so great about this style of helping is that you put the ball in the other person's court to solve his or her own problem. Your job is not to fix things, but to create the kind of relationship and interactions that are conducive for a person to solve his or her own problems.

Facing Silence

People "speak" in many different ways, often with words, but also with their nonverbal behavior, facial expressions, and body language. Silences can mean many different things, depending on the situation. Some silences are productive and useful, in that people are thinking about stuff, personalizing previous points that were made, and reflecting on where and how they want to go next. Other times, silences can signal confusion or resistance. Your first step will be to make sense of the silence and decide whether it requires some sort of intervention (clarification, probe, structure) or whether it is best to let things sit for a while.

Beginning helpers often feel the need to fill every silence with another question, and they tend to talk too much out of nervousness. Although it is true that silences can sometimes last far too long, you do not want to get in the habit of rescuing people every time the conversation lapses. Instead, you want the client to feel responsible for what happens. It is thus a critical relationship skill to refrain from talking at times, to let silences ferment, and to communicate that it is not your job to keep things going.

Depending on what the silence means, you might do one thing or another, attempting to address the underlying communication: resentment, anger, confusion, enlightenment, or whatever. Generally speaking, the best course of action to take when you face silence is to wait it out (unless you are reasonably certain that something else is going on that requires more forceful intervention). Not only will this give you time to plan your next move, but it lets the other person know that he or she is the one that must move things forward. For this strategy to work, however, you must not only keep your mouth shut, but also appear as if you are relaxed, unconcerned, and willing to be endlessly patient. This is not an easy task when you are actually churning inside, on the edge of panic, screaming inside your head: "Say something, damn it! Why are you just sitting there?"

Resist the impulse to do something. Take a deep breath. Study the situation. Wait to see what unfolds.

There is a point, obviously, when it's clear that the other person intends to outwait you. There may be a game going on, a competition for control, or as was mentioned earlier, perhaps the person just doesn't understand what you expect or what you want.

Next, you can try reflecting what is going on, or what you believe is going on: "You don't seem to have much to say."

Because you might still face more silence after that remark, especially with someone who is being resistant, you'd better be ready with your next response. Don't worry, though: During the passing minutes, you have plenty of time to rehearse what to say next. I've lived through 45 consecutive minutes of complete silence (except for a few grunts) from some especially surly adolescents.

Next, you can try leading things in another direction: "Let's move on to another topic because this one seems done." If that doesn't work, there is always something else you can try. There is no single, foolproof strategy to use with silence, except to remember that it can be useful, as well as excruciatingly endless. You will find it helpful to increase your tolerance for silence, withholding the urge to fill every space with noise.

Establishing Goals

You've been listening and exploring for a while. You have reflected the content and feelings you've heard. You probed areas that seemed especially important. You asked relevant questions to gather needed information. You've worked on building a solid alliance. You have assessed the risk potential. You have some preliminary diagnostic impressions.

Unless all the preceding activity has taken place in a single meeting, then you have also had time to do some homework. You've consulted some books and colleagues about what you've learned. They have probably gotten you thinking about other areas to explore further, as well as other possibilities of what might be happening with your client.

Now it is time to move the person to some sort of goal definition. Given that these problems are present and that you know something about their origins and effects, what does the person want to do about them? You can be unhappy in a relationship and decide on a number of different courses of action: You want to make things the way they were, you want out, you want to resolve the present struggles but not get into other areas, you want to use the current issue as a means to make the relationships stronger, or maybe even you decide not to do anything at all at this time. In any case, you need to help the person clarify what it is that is desired most. Keep in mind that there is usually more than one goal that is possible.

When helping people set goals for themselves, there are a few things to consider:

1. *Make the goals specific.* Unless you can specify what the person will do, when he or she will do it, how often, and in what circumstances, it's difficult to tell whether it was accomplished. For someone who says that he wants more control over his life, you might help him declare more specifically that he intends to exercise more control over his eating patterns. In particular, he agrees to restrict himself to a calorie intake of 1,500 per day, six out of seven days.

2. *Make the goals realistic.* There is nothing more discouraging then setting a goal that can't be attained. You want to build successful experiences for people, as much as possible. Help establish successive, baby steps toward the ultimate objective. If someone has not exercised a single day in the previous months, it is a setup for failure to construct the goal of working out for an

hour every day. It's far better to start in smaller, bite-size pieces, perhaps walking for a minimum of 20 minutes, three times per week. If the person goes beyond what was agreed, all the better, but at least there is a greater likelihood that it will be accomplished.

3. *Make sure the goals declared are actually relevant to the major issue.* In your zeal to help the person come up with something concrete (like a diet or exercise program), you may miss the salient point of the struggle. Ideally, the goal should reflect some sort of action taken that is connected to what was discussed. For instance, a child has not been completing her homework on a regular basis because of feelings that her efforts are wasted and that she'll never get into college or even find a decent job. It would probably not be appropriate to urge this child to commit herself to turning in homework assignments when the real issue has to do with motivation. Perhaps in this case, the goal might be related to finding evidence to support or refute her erroneous assumption that the future is hopeless. This might not be as specific as a commitment to turn in homework assignments two out of five days, but it does address more closely the deeper problems that need to be explored.

4. *Negotiate the goals as a team.* One mistake beginners often make is being too directive and prescriptive: "Maybe what you could do after the session is go home and talk to your parents about what you have decided." That might very well be an excellent idea, but people tend not to be as committed to following through on assignments given to them by others, rather than those they come up with on their own (with a little help from you). I don't know how many times I've heard clients return to the next session with an apologetic grin and say, "Gee, I'm sorry. I forgot to do the homework you gave me." I am then quick to correct this misperception: "Excuse me. But I didn't *give* you that homework. *You* decided that was what you wanted to do. But I guess you changed your mind, huh?" I love being able to throw that back at them, that their failure to follow through is a choice they made, not a way to get back at me because they are feeling pushed.

It may take you a bit longer to negotiate goals with a client, but in the long run, it's worth it so it's clear that the choice to meet the goals or not is up to the person. At the same time, you are also teaching the client how to do this for himself or herself in the future. One of the general goals of counseling is to help people to learn the process so they can internalize the procedures in such a way that they don't need to come running back every time they have another problem in the future.

The negotiated goal-setting dialogue would involve the use of all the skills we've covered so far:

Helper: "So far, we've covered a lot of ground talking about your reluctance to be assertive with others, especially authority figures. We've also talked about how you learned to be this way from watching your parents in action. How would you summarize what we've done?" [Open-ended question asking the client to continue summarizing]

Client: "That's about it, I guess. Plus I thought it was interesting the way being so unwilling to stand up for myself has held me back from so many opportunities."

Helper: "There are actually a few other things you mentioned as well— problems at work, uncertainty about the future, concerns about your mother's failing health—but let's concentrate first on that issue of being assertive." [More summarizing; focusing]

Client: "Sounds good."

Helper: "Okay, so what would you like to do before I see you next?"

The helper realizes that what clients do between sessions to act on what they've learned is probably more important than the talks themselves, which are designed primarily to promote constructive changes. Using another open-ended question, she gets the client thinking about how to convert a general discussion into some specific action that can be taken.

Client: "I don't know."

This is such a typical response! Most people don't, in fact, know what to do or how to do it; if they did, they wouldn't have solicited help in the first place. Be prepared for this less-than-encouraging answer:

Helper: "I was just thinking about some ways you could apply what we've been talking about to your life."

Client: [Blank look]

Helper: "We need to come up with something you can do this week that would help you feel like you were making progress toward being more assertive in your life."

Notice the use of the pronoun, "we," making clear that *we* are working on this together: *You* are not alone. Slowly, the helper is introducing the idea that it will be expected for the client to do something constructive.

Client: "I guess I could . . . I'm not really sure . . ."

Helper: "You're finding this hard to do. It's like you want to do a good job with this, but you don't want to disappoint me."

Client: [Looks away, then down at the floor, shuffling feet, obviously uncomfortable]

This is a good use of reflecting feelings, taking the time to hear and respond to the client's fear of failure. It's entirely possible, if there was time (which there often isn't), to detour for a little while and explore these feelings further. Because time is limited, the helper pushes further:

Helper: "I know this is hard the first time we do this. What I'm hoping we can do is work together to come up with something you could do, something that would help you to feel that you are really changing your old patterns."

Client: [Looks up hesitantly] "You mean, like, maybe I should go up to mother and tell her I don't appreciate her meddling so much in my life?"

This strikes you as a ridiculously improbable idea. It would never work. This client has never stood up to his mother before, and you know it isn't a norm in this family to speak out like that. You want to lead the client to settling on a goal that is much more realistic and attainable:

Helper: "Yeah, something like that. I was wondering, though, if you could think of something that might be a little easier to tackle the first time."

Client: [Laughs]

Helper: "You know, maybe something to do with your best friend you were talking about."

The helper does have a general idea of where she wants to lead her client and the kind of goal she wants him to come up with. But rather than taking the easy route of just prescribing the homework, she's guiding him to come up with it himself. Granted, this does take longer. But you are training the client to think in new ways. You are teaching new skills for how to (a) define a problem, (b) establish incremental goals, and then (c) follow through on commitments. You will make this a normal part of your work with people, so they regularly come to expect that all future sessions will end with an invitation to summarize what was discussed, then to translate this conversation into some sort of action that can be completed before the next meeting. This also suggests the way you would begin all subsequent sessions—by asking the person to report on how things went. If the goal was reached, you can reinforce that behavior and move on to the next issue or the next incremental step toward the ultimate objective. If, however, the goal wasn't reached, then you can explore further what happened, and what that means.

There are several reasons why people don't complete their goals:

1. The goals weren't their goals in the first place, but they agreed with them to please you.

2. They are acting out toward you, punishing you in some way, by sabotaging themselves.

3. They decided that the goals weren't so important after all.

4. They faced unanticipated roadblocks that they couldn't overcome.

5. They became fearful of the consequences of acting and felt unwilling to accept the responsibility for this.

6. They were actively sabotaged by others in their lives who were threatened by the changes that were anticipated.

You would be amazed how often this last reason occurs. Friends and family members may very well declare passionately that they want your client to get better, but secretly they have their own agendas. If your client does change and become more assertive, for example, then it means others will have to make corresponding adjustments as well. Because this is hard work, it's often easier to undermine the person who is trying to break loose.

One warning: People will return with lots of excuses and reasons why they couldn't complete their goals. Don't take it personally, and don't accept the excuses. Most often, people will try to blame others or things outside of themselves for things not going the way they prefer. "It was the weather," or "I didn't have time," or "You wouldn't believe what happened" are common excuses. All you can do when confronted by such defensiveness is shrug, try to get the person to accept some responsibility for the failure, and then retrench and start again. At times, you will just have to let things go and conclude (based on consistent failure to complete declared goals) that the person isn't yet ready to move toward action. It may be time to continue with more exploration until the time is ripe. Meanwhile, you will need to stifle your own impatience and need for action: People change at their own pace, not yours!

Making the Transition to Action

Setting goals acts as a bridge between the exploration process described in this chapter and the action phase presented in the next one. It is one thing to help people understand their problems and gain insight into their origins, and it's another to motivate them to do something about the issues they are now aware of.

You will likely lose a few people at this point. Some individuals don't mind talking about things, but when it comes to taking decisive action, they would rather keep things the way they are. Even if life isn't ideal, at least it's reasonably predictable. The unknown is terrifying.

In some cases, you will have to recognize that this is as far as your client is ready to go. Accept this. Deal with your own need for action. Take steps to make it easy for the person to continue sessions at a future time.

"I notice that you seem reluctant to take action right now," you might begin. "That's fine," you reassure the person further. "You certainly have plenty to think about. We have covered a lot of ground rather quickly. You need time to digest all this, to make some decisions. You seem to realize that if you do initiate some action, it will set in motion a number of other consequences, a few of which you aren't sure if you want to deal with."

You may notice relief on the person's face at this point. In one sense, you are letting him or her off the hook, but in another, you are respecting his or her pace rather than imposing your own. "I just want you to know," you continue, "that whenever you're ready to take things further, I'm ready and available to help you do so." Now you have left the door open for future collaborations.

Assuming the client is ready to talk about goals and putting into practice what was understood and articulated, the next step is to prepare the person for the next stage. Lots of reassurance and support is important at this critical juncture. You may even wish to offer some feedback at this point, sharing your impressions about what you see and sense is going on. This is a good time for a summary as well, something along the lines as the following:

> We seem to be at a point where you will have to decide what you want to do. You've said several times that you are quite unhappy with the way things are in your life, but I also sense that you aren't sure you know what you want to do about that yet. Perhaps it might be useful for us to sort out which specific things you are prepared to change right now versus those you are still thinking about. Where would you like to start?

Thus begins the transition toward action. Although not all the people you try to help even need to move toward resolution of specific problems, it still helps to think in terms of where you can help people act on what they have learned. One of the criticisms about counseling, or any educational process, is that results don't often generalize from one situation to others. That means it's your job to help people apply what they are realizing and learning to as many contexts as possible.

For Review

- Thorough exploration must be completed before undertaking any action strategy.
- Internal attitudes and attending behaviors are used to stay focused and communicate interest and compassion.
- The most important helping skill involves listening actively and reflecting back what was heard.
- If you must ask direct questions, structure them so they are open ended and elicit maximum information.
- When responding to people, find a balance between attention to content and feelings.
- Whenever possible, goals should be specific, realistic, mutually negotiated, and relevant to the client's main concerns.

For Reflection and Practice

1. Record yourself practicing basic helping skills. Pay close attention to the things you do best, as well as weaknesses. Use the checklists in this chapter to compare your performance with what is most desirable. Review the tape with your instructor or an experienced helper who can provide you with feedback and suggestions for improvement.

2. Next time you are in a social situation with friends or family, introduce the idea of asking one another open-ended questions that are designed to promote greater intimacy. Take turns asking one another questions, or allow one person to take the "hot seat" until the point at which he or she is "stumped" by a question or refuses to answer.

3. Watch or listen to media interviewers on television and radio, paying particular attention to their exploration and questioning skills. Note what they do that cuts off communication as well as their methods that seem to elicit the most revealing information.

4. Get together with partners from class and practice the exploration skills in this chapter, giving each other feedback on what you liked best and least.

5. Set goals for yourself following the structure presented in the chapter. Once you feel comfortable with the process, practice goal setting with a willing partner who would like to make some changes.

6. Go to the library and view demonstration videos of counseling and therapy sessions in action. Some of the most prominent practitioners have been recorded for teaching purposes. Get some recommendations from your instructor (and others) as to which are the best samples for beginners to watch.

7. Ask experienced helpers to conduct an exploration interview with you as the client. Debrief them afterward about what they did and why.

For Further Reading

Brew, L., & Kottler, J. A. (2008). *Applied helping skills: Transforming lives.* Thousand Oaks, CA: Sage.

DeSole, L. M. (2006). *Making contact: The therapist's guide to conducting a successful first interview.* Boston: Pearson.

Drummond, R., & Jones, K. D. (2006). *Assessment procedures for counselors and helping professionals* (6th ed.). Upper Saddle River, NJ: Prentice Hall.

Halstead, R. W. (2007). *Assessment of client core issues.* Alexandria, VA: American Counseling Association.

Hood, A. B., & Johnson, R. W. (2007). *Assessment in counseling: A guide to the use of psychological assessment procedures* (4th ed.). Alexandria, VA: American Counseling Association.

Kanel, K. (2007). *A guide to crisis intervention* (3rd ed.). Thomson Brooks/Cole.

McHenry, B., & McHenry, J. (2007). *What therapists say and why they say it.* Boston: Pearson.

Neukrug, E. S., & Schwitzer, A. M. (2006). *Skills and tools for today's counselors and psychologists.* Belmont, CA: Wadsworth.

Peterson, C. (2006). *A primer of positive psychology.* New York: Oxford University Press.

Snyder, C. R., & Lopez, S. J. (2006). *Positive psychology: The scientific and practical explorations of human strengths.* Thousand Oaks, CA: Sage.

6

Action Skills

People tend to move at their own speed, usually much slower than you would prefer. When you sense some reluctance or balking on the part of someone, your job may be to facilitate greater readiness. You can do this by continuing further exploration, by taking a break from sessions to give the person time to process and reflect on matters, or by moving ahead at a cautious pace. Regardless of which course you choose, remember that you must monitor your own impatience carefully so that you do not push someone to do something for which he or she does not yet feel ready. One of the most common mistakes of beginners involves pushing too hard and fast toward action before doing sufficient exploration that leads to goal setting.

A Check-Off List

Assuming that it is both appropriate and timely to move from exploration to action, there are several steps you must take in preparation. Thinking of this like a pilot's check-off list, consulted just before takeoff, review the following items to make sure everything is operational before you launch into action:

- *Is the relationship solid enough to sustain perceived assaults?* Has sufficient trust been developed that the relationship can sustain some degree of confrontation? You will want to assess carefully how hard you can push and how far.
- *Have you conducted sufficient exploration and gathered enough information to get a handle on where you are headed?* You will probably notice deficiencies

after you get started. It will occur to you in the middle of your efforts that maybe you need to stop for a bit and find out more about what is going on. You will say something to yourself like, "Gee, I'm about to ask this person to follow through on changing interaction patterns with family members and I don't know nearly enough about what is going on. Time to get some more data."

- *Are you clear about a working diagnosis of what is going on so you can target interventions appropriately?* Make sure that you aren't forging ahead, just for movement's sake, without having some goals in mind.

- *Have you recruited the assistance or support of significant others in the person's life so he or she doesn't sabotage efforts to change?* Remember that all your best efforts can be wiped out unless you've been successful in recruiting support in the client's world. You will only see this person for a hour or a little more each week, but many others exert tremendous influence for hours every day.

- *Are the goals you've established realistic, specific, and attainable in the time parameters?* Remind yourself to check continuously whether what you are asking of someone can actually be done.

- *Is the treatment plan respectful of and consistent with the cultural values of the person you are helping?* Be very careful that you aren't imposing your values about what you think is good for people without considering the client's unique world.

- *Are you prepared to throw out your agenda if things don't work out as anticipated?* This last item suggests that a certain degree of fluidity and flexibility is needed when beginning an action plan: Things don't often go as you anticipated. In fact, some of the best work you will do occurs at a level beyond your awareness, much less your intentions. Do all the planning you have time for. Consult with supervisors and more experienced practitioners about what you intend to do. Solicit as much input as you can. Map out your strategy. Then be prepared to throw it all away and go with the flow.

Taking Action

Action can take place at a number of different levels, some of them observable and some of them either invisible or with delayed effects. Regardless of what you contract with your clients to do, you want them to be accountable, mostly to themselves, for following through on their commitments. Here are some examples of the kinds of action that might be taken as part of a helping relationship:

- "I'm going to write in my journal for 15 minutes each evening before I go to bed, reviewing what I did during the day that I feel especially proud of."
- "At least three times per day that I become aware I am exaggerating how bad things appear, I will stop myself and substitute more positive alternatives."

- "It's time for me to stop procrastinating about telling my brother how I feel about his attempts to control my life."
- "For me, it would be a major accomplishment to *not* plan anything for Sunday."
- "I need to think more about this issue related to my fear of failure. I'm going to talk to some of my friends to see if they have noticed ways that I hold myself back."
- "This is it! I'm ready! Before I see you next time, I will have filed for divorce."
- "I'm going to practice the relaxation exercise I just learned. I can think of several different situations when it would help me to stay calm."
- "Next weekend, I'm going to get away by myself. I need to sit down, alone, without distractions or outside influences, and plan what I want to do with my life."

This sampling of goals demonstrates the assortment of actions that could be structured. Changes can take place both internally or externally. In the former, the client might use imagery to rehearse new patterns or focus on certain thoughts and feelings that get in the way. In the latter, specific behaviors are highlighted, acted on, and then evaluated. You will want to tailor the particular kind of action taken to the needs of the client.

Planning an Intervention

During training experiences, it is not unusual for helpers to work with people in front of one-way mirrors, behind which there are whole teams of consultants available to reflect on the proceedings, make suggestions, and discuss the implications of each choice. Unfortunately, most of us work in somewhat less than ideal circumstances in which we operate alone or with little supervision. Nevertheless, you can still create a number of opportunities to consult with others during the stage of treatment planning. Even if you don't have access to formal review conferences or staff meetings in which cases can be thoroughly reviewed, you can still solicit feedback from professionals who have more experience. You will also have time to read some literature related to your case, as well as talk to others with similar problems who might have some valuable input.

The way all this comes together is something like this: (a) Your initial interview is completed; (b) you panic, wondering how the heck you can possibly help this person when you barely know what is going on; (c) you run, not walk, to the library, bookshelves, or Internet to gather as much information as you can about the type of complaint presented; (d) you talk to trusted confidantes to get their advice on the matter; (e) you look around for others you know who have had some experience in this area; and (f) you go to a supervisor for advice (after you've already done your preliminary home-work so you don't look too stupid). Once you've completed these steps, then you are *probably* ready (you will rarely ever feel ready) to begin planning your first interventions.

Generally, you will want to think through, if not write down, the following:

- What is the problem you wish to address first?
- How is this related to the initial diagnosis and presenting complaints?
- What intervention or strategy is likely to produce desired outcomes?
- What can you do if that doesn't work?
- How will you know whether your intervention was successful?

In a third session with a defiant teenager, we have agreed that it would be in his best interests to extricate himself from continued involvement in a neighborhood gang that has been responsible for a number of crimes in the area. The first problem to attack will be to figure out how he can remove him-self from this situation and replace his time with more constructive activities.

His initial diagnosis of "oppositional disorder" appears to be a situational manifestation of his behavior. In fact, from exploration into his background, it has been determined that he can be quite cooperative, even eager to be helpful, in some areas of his life.

The first thing it might be useful to do is to *reframe* (redefine in a more useful way) his behavior from being "oppositional" or a "gangster" to being "fiercely loyal to old friends." This puts his behavior in a more functional, positive light; rather than labeling him as pathological, the emphasis instead is on his personal responsibility and free choice.

It will be important to develop a strong mentoring—even parental—relationship with him in which he can be guided to make new choices for role models other than leaders of his gang. I don't want him to feel the least criticism or judgment from me; on the contrary, I will use reflective listening skills to help him express his feelings and thoughts.

I am thinking that it might also be helpful for him to participate in some sort of athletic activities associated with school (he claims to be a natural athlete, especially good at soccer and track—the best in his gang, which is why he was the one often saddled with the task of outrunning police). I won't suggest these activities to him but instead guide him gently in that direction. If he seems resistant to athletics, then we can brainstorm other extracurricular activities and employment opportunities that will help him structure his time more productively.

Ultimately, I will know if my efforts have been useful when he disen-gages from gang activity, learns alternative ways to express his anger and disappointment, and behaves in more socially responsible ways. I have summarized this treatment plan in my notes as follows:

Goal	Intervention
Reduce gang activity	Find other social outlets
Explore unexpressed rage	Reflect underlying feelings
Promote understanding	Use relationship as leverage to build trust and intimacy
Build new social contacts	Arrange for extracurricular activities
Promote responsibility	Make him accountable for structure of sessions
Change negative messages	Teach new ways to think about his future possibilities
Decrease acting out	Negotiate consequences for lapses in judgment

Contracting for Change

Sometimes you will find it useful, even necessary, to formalize the action plan that has been developed. This strategy is especially well-suited to any situation in which you can define specific behaviors in need of changing. Again, I want to stress that you don't wish to make the person accountable to you for the outcome, but rather to himself or herself. That way you do not get caught up in power games in which the person may try to punish you by hurting himself or herself.

During negotiations for a "self-contract," you act as the scribe to write down exactly what the person will do, when it will be done, how often, with whom, and under what circumstances, as well as what will happen under various scenarios if the goals are not met, partially met, or fully attained.

Let's assume, for example, that you are working with someone who has problems saving money, often wasting limited resources on frivolous indulgences that leave little left over for meeting basic needs like food and bus fare. You discover during your exploration that the young woman enjoys most in life going to movies when her budget allows it. Furthermore, you have learned that what she dreads the most is cleaning her bathroom, a chore she puts off as long as possible.

So far you have been able to identify a target behavior to change (saving money), as well as contingency reinforcers that are both rewarding (movies) and aversive (cleaning bathrooms). From this basic information, you can then help the woman write a self-contract.

Self-Contract

I agree to develop a budget for the next week in which I will keep at least $600 in my bank account at all times. In addition, I will not spend more than $50 on any purchases other than basic necessities. If I reach this goal by the end of the week, then I will be allowed to go to two matinees or one evening movie, plus I'm permitted to reward myself with a gift not to exceed $20.

If I do not meet my declared goals, I agree that I will not go to any movies. Second (Ugh!), I will clean my bathroom completely for a minimum of one hour.

| _____ | _____ |
| Signed | Date |

Because it is quite common that people will not do what they say they will do, it is very important to build in mechanisms for recovery. Do not let people provide excuses or blame others for the lack of movement. Following a reality therapy–based approach, it is better to talk about personal choices that were made rather than failures. It is also useful to discuss "self-discipline" strategies rather than "punishment" when the person does not comply with goals stated in the contract. This terminology again reinforces the notion that certain consequences result from personal choices that are made.

Confrontation

There is little doubt that this is one of the most difficult skills to use well. Some beginners avoid confronting people for fear of hurting their feelings or saying something rude or harmful. The opposite is also a problem—those who jump in and say what they think, but at a level that is hurtful or pushes people away.

Confrontation is best employed whenever you observe some discrepancy or inconsistency. This can occur between

- *What a person is saying versus doing.* "I'm confused. You say that you're not good at expressing yourself, but you've spent the past 20 minutes pouring your heart out."
- *What a person says now versus what was said earlier.* "Wait a minute. Didn't you tell me last time that family pressure is what held you back from finding a career? Now, you're saying you didn't have the smarts."

- *How a person behaves now versus earlier.* "You seem to be acting so angry and hurt over the way you were treated even though last time you said it didn't bother you at all."
- *What the person reports versus what has been reported by others.* "You say that you do not have a drinking problem, but your probation officer says that you have been arrested three times for driving while intoxicated."

Another kind of confrontation, called *immediacy,* focuses on something you are aware of in the present: "You have been describing yourself as unable to take care of yourself, but I notice right now you seem to be doing an excellent job of doing so. I find myself respecting you even more when you stand up for yourself like this."

Finally, you may decide to confront people when they engage in behavior that violates boundaries established or involves destructive behavior: "We agreed that as long as we were working together, you wouldn't use alcohol or drugs, but you aren't able to live up to this promise. That is not acceptable."

It is apparent that there are times when your job involves providing honest, clear, and straightforward feedback regarding particular behaviors. You are not being critical of a person, but rather of certain behaviors. You are showing a high degree of sensitivity and diplomacy. After all, unless you can figure out a way to tell someone that what he or she is doing is not a good thing, and do it in a way that can be heard, then you are wasting time and energy. Worse yet, you will drive the person away.

When you offer feedback to someone, keep the following guidelines in mind:

1. *Include both supportive and critical features.* Start out by offering something positive about what you observe. Then include something you can think of that would be helpful for the person to know. For example, "When you tell people you're not very good at something, just like you did with me, you end up diminishing yourself in such a way that you aren't taken seriously."

2. *Be specific.* Feedback that is too general is next to useless, even though it might seem to have substance. Instead of telling someone that he has a problem with authority figures, it would be far better to tell him that he has a problem acting out toward older adults in positions of direct power, especially those who seem arrogant and pushy.

3. *Provide supporting examples.* Make your feedback come alive for the person, in a way that is hard to write off: "I've noticed that whenever someone tries to get close, you do everything in your power to get that person to

reject you. You did this with me during our initial meetings when you kept complaining so much, and you've done that repeatedly with your team members at work."

4. *Be sensitive.* What you are offering to the person may be very threatening. Try to frame what you are saying in a way that is diplomatic and caring. Offer it from a place of love in your heart: People are much more likely to hear threatening material when it's offered in a spirit of caring rather than when they perceive it as a personal attack. If, at any time during the intervention, you observe or feel the person pulling away or feeling hurt, then abandon what you are doing and return to active listening skills to reflect the strong feelings: "I noticed that earlier when I was telling you that sometimes it's hard to be around you when you act accusingly, you seemed to be startled, as if you felt wounded by what I was telling you."

With any sort of confrontation or feedback, make certain to be as supportive as you can. It tends to be a dramatic intervention, one that sparks a lot of movement. Because it is so potent, however, you want to be careful and cautious in its application.

Teaching People to Think Differently

There is a form of cognitive therapy that teaches people to change the ways they think about their predicaments. Often useful in single-session doses, you introduce an alternative way to interpret a situation, often substituting more rational patterns. Essentially, this action method follows the message of the children's rhyme, "Sticks and stones may break my bones, but names can never hurt me." In other words, how you feel inside does not depend on what other people say or do, or what happens to you, but rather what you say to yourself—how you choose to interpret things.

Make no mistake: This is a very powerful idea, one that can often result in immediate relief of symptoms, especially when someone is feeling sorry for himself, exaggerating a situation, or otherwise blowing things out of proportion. Recall earlier in the book there was the case of the man who was very angry—make that enraged—because someone cut him off on the highway. He believed that his intense feelings of anger, fear, resentment, and indignation were the result of what this errant driver did to him. In actuality, although such a situation would never be pleasant, or even a neutral experience, what made it so disruptive in his life was not what happened, but what he *imagined* occurred. Believe me: There is a huge difference.

If the man was telling himself something along the lines of, "I can't believe the son of a bitch did this to me! Who does he think he is?" then the logical result might very well be extreme agitation (rate that a 9 or 10). If, on the other hand, he chose to think to himself, "This is certainly annoying. But I realize that this wasn't personal. Stuff like this happens, and it's best to protect myself as best I can, learn from the experience, and then move along," then quite a different reaction would result. In the second case, he might still feel upset, but this time only a 2 or 3, a much more reasonable reaction to a not-uncommon occurrence.

When you face someone who is upset about something, and this person genuinely wants to stop feeling this way, you can offer a method to alter the negative emotion by changing the irrational thought pattern. Such dysfunctional beliefs come in two basic forms:

1. *Demands that the world be a particular way.* "It's not fair!" is a frequent refrain. Another example is when someone becomes unreasonably disappointed when others don't act the way he or she thinks they should. In fact, look for lots of "shoulds" or "musts" in the person's verbalizations, as in, "She should have been there," or "He must come through for me." What makes these statements so erroneous is that they are based on the assumption that you are the center of the universe and that others must live by your rules.

2. *Gross exaggerations of reality.* "It's awful that this happened" or "This is terrible that this happened to me" are common manifestations of this irrational symptom. In each case, the person distorts what is going on, viewing the significance or consequences of the event as a disaster. Is it really the end of the world because you didn't get what you wanted? Does it seem like a reasonable response to be immobilized just because things didn't work out? Is it truly a disaster that this happened, or more likely, that this is only an inconvenience, a minor setback, or a small disappointment?

Employing this action strategy, what you attempt to do is confront someone with the irrational beliefs that are getting in the way of clear-headed thinking. You introduce alternative ways of interpreting the situation that are more logical, or at least more based in reality. You might say to someone who is feeling sorry for herself over a rude comment made her way,

> I understand that you are feeling hurt that you were told you are unattractive. But just because this person may see you this way doesn't mean that's the way you really are. Isn't it possible that he is wrong, or misguided, or has a different standard of attractiveness than you or others might subscribe to? And even

if he is right—let's say that almost everyone agrees that you are unattractive—what would that mean? That your life is over?

Hopefully, you can get a feel for the engaging, dramatic nature of this dialogue in which you challenge people's thinking about their predicaments. You push them to look at their assumptions, to see if they are based on sound and rational ideas, and then to select alternative interpretations that will produce distinctly different emotional reactions.

When first learning and teaching this method, you will find it useful to write out the process according to the following steps:

1. *What is the situation that you believe is making you upset?* This question is carefully worded. This situation isn't really making the person feel anything at all; this is something the person is doing to himself or herself: "I got a C– on my paper in school. I worked hard on this assignment and I still got this terrible grade."

2. *What are you feeling in response to this situation?* People are never feeling just one thing, but many different reactions, so get an exhaustive list. It is also helpful to rate on a 1 to 10 scale just how intense the feeling is so that you have a way to measure changes that took place after your intervention:

- I'm feeling depressed. I've give it about an 8 because I worked so hard on this.
- I'm also pretty angry about this. Make that a 9.
- I'd also say it's a 7 for confusion. I don't understand what I did wrong.
- I'm scared too, very scared, because now I might need to rethink what I'm doing. Another 9.

All throughout his process, of course, you are using your exploration skills to reflect the feelings being expressed and draw out others that might not be immediately apparent.

3. *What are the underlying thoughts behind these reactions?* Because according to this approach, it's assumed that negative feelings stem from irrational thoughts, you want to uncover what those might be. Look for variations of the themes, "It's not fair," "I can't stand this," "This is awful," and "It shouldn't be like this."

You will get some resistance at this point. Remember, you are introducing another way to think about things. In spite of what people say, that they would love to be free of their debilitating symptoms, most don't want to invest the hard work involved in making significant changes. It's far easier to blame others or circumstances outside your control than to accept responsibility for your own troubles.

If you have done your homework (which may involve more reading on this approach) and stick with it, you will likely uncover several irrational beliefs.

- Because I got a C– on this paper, I'm not very smart and I'll never do well.
- This guy is a real idiot for giving me this grade. He never should have been so unclear in the first place about what he wanted.
- I may as well give up and try something else since I can't get a decent grade.

4. *Confront the irrational beliefs.* It may be somewhat obvious what is irrational about the preceding statements. Where is the evidence that just because she got a C– on one paper, she is a hopeless student? How does she know that she'll never do well just because of one grade that was below her expectations? What is it about a C– anyway that makes it a "horrible" grade rather than simply one that is about average? And what is the connection between doing less than expected on one sample of behavior and then concluding that the course she is following is not the right one?

There may be other reasons why she is considering a switch in directions, but if that main rationale is based on these erroneous beliefs and exaggerated reactions, then she is not looking at things very clearly. Once she examines her interpretations of this disappointing situation, she may elect to change her view of things. "Okay, this is a setback. But it doesn't have to be a big deal, unless I make it one. This grade of a C– is not the best I could get, but neither is it the worst. I could learn from this situation and do much better the next time, especially if I take the time to read the teacher better and find out more specifically what he is looking for. I may not like this situation, but I can easily live with it. It isn't terrible, just a little disappointing."

5. *Measure the changes.* The last step involves going back to reassess the effect of this method. Take each of the feelings identified in Step 3 and rate them again on a 1 to 10 scale, substituting the new thinking patterns for the old ones.

The goal of this method is not necessarily to reduce all emotional reactions, which is both unreasonable and perhaps undesirable. Instead, you are giving the person a choice as to how she wants to react to any given situation. Nobody is going to feel good about setbacks or disappointments or tragic situations, but you can moderate your responses if that is what you would prefer.

Feeling	Before	After
Depression	8	2

"I'm not feeling depressed any more. Maybe just a tiny bit down."

Anger	9	5

"I'm still kind of angry. I don't think he was very clear about what he expected."

Confusion	7	3

"I also feel a little confused about the assignment but not much at all about what this paper means in the context of my life."

Fear	9	1

"No, I don't feel afraid any more. The only thing I am the least apprehensive about is how to go about telling this teacher what I think about his grading system."

Constructing Alternative Stories

A similar but distinctly different approach to promoting radical changes in the ways people view themselves and their worlds comes from narrative therapy. Although this strategy also seeks to promote alternative interpretations of reality, its focus is less on individually created irrational beliefs and more on how perceptions are shaped by the larger, dominant culture, often without your consent or active participation. This would be especially true for members of ethnic minorities and other oppressed groups who learn to accept certain "narratives" about the way things are in the world. Instead, this approach, like others that are labeled as constructivist because they help people construct alternative views, helps people see that many different realities are possible.

A woman comes to you with a story about the way things are, or at least one view of that reality. She believes that she is not cut out for advanced education, that she was lucky to even graduate high school. "Women in my family don't go to college," she insists. "My mother always cleaned houses, and I guess that's what I'll do too." It is clear, therefore, that this woman subscribes to a particular story about who she is and what her place is in the world. This narrative was created not so much from her own conscious choices as it was constructed from certain images handed down to her by her family, by her perceived gender and socioeconomic roles, and even by media that reinforced notions about her designated lot in life.

Instead of disputing her beliefs as irrational, you might instead help her examine the origins of her particular story about who she is. How was this narrative shaped to become part of who she believed she is? One strategy employed, *externalizing the problem,* seeks to differentiate the person from the problem in such a way that blame and shame are avoided. Instead of saying to herself, "I'm stupid," the problem, "stupid," is referred to in language that makes it clear that it isn't really part of her. You might ask her, for example, "When did 'stupid' first take over your life and fool you into thinking that was you?"

Essentially, you are helping the person to coauthor an alternative story, one in which she feels more empowered and less a victim of circumstances she can't control. Although this whole method is quite complex and takes considerable training, on the most basic level, you might use it to promote action by asking your clients the following questions:

- "How did it happen that this problem managed to infiltrate your life and make it so difficult for you to get what you want?" Notice the way the problem is externalized, as if it is the enemy to be defeated.
- "When was a time recently when you were able to ignore the temptations of the problem?" This strategy of "looking for exceptions" offers some balance to the situation, because it reinforces the idea that the client can exercise some control.
- "What is another way that we could view your situation so that you will feel more inclined to act in your best interests?" The very basis of this question implies that reality can be changed according to alternative perceptions. This is a very powerful idea that can be quite motivating when someone feels stuck or hopeless.

Role Playing and Rehearsal

One of the things that helping is designed for is providing opportunities to practice new behaviors in a safe setting and to make adjustments in preparation for the outside world. This might actually be one of the most important components of promoting action in client behavior, that is, directing a dress rehearsal in preparation for the live performance.

You cannot just talk about being assertive and then put people out into the world to try it out. You cannot describe some new skill or strategy and then suggest that someone start using it immediately. Not only is there usually some resistance to experimenting with anything that is unknown or perceived as risky, but people are more likely to fail in their efforts without some systematic coaching.

Rehearsal strategies are designed to simulate anticipated situations, then to try out a new behavior, evaluating its relative effectiveness. If, for example, a person wants to confront a boss, parent, or friend, you might take on the role of the antagonist and play out the scenario as it would likely unfold realistically. At times, you could stop the action and provide feedback, as illustrated in this dialogue between a helper and a boy who believes he is being treated unfairly by his teacher:

Helper: "Instead of just talking about what you might say to your teacher, show me."

Boy: "Huh?"

Helper: "I'll pretend I'm your teacher and you talk to me the way you would to her."

Boy: "What do you mean?"

The instructions are actually quite clear but the boy is reluctant, maybe embarrassed, to act things out. This is a very common reaction so you have to be persistent, assuming that you aren't shoving this down his throat:

Helper: "Let's rehearse a little what you might say to her. That way you'll have some practice. And maybe I can make a few suggestions that will be useful."

Boy: [Nods his head a little apprehensively]

Helper: "You're a little uncomfortable with this, huh?"

It isn't a bad move to reflect the feelings displayed in the nonverbal behavior. This will ensure that the boy participates willingly in the exchange. Remember: You don't want to pressure people to do things they don't feel ready to do.

Boy: "I'm okay. Go on."

Helper: "I'll be your teacher. Show me how she talks and acts."

You can't realistically play a role unless you know something about the character. Rather than asking the person to tell you about the antagonist, have him show you. This actually accomplishes two things at the same time. First, you get the information you need by seeing the way the other person behaves, making it easier for you to imitate the style. Second, when the client is forced to become his nemesis, he often develops an empathic connection to the point where he can understand the other's point of view:

Boy: "Well, she kind of sits real still, with her hands in her lap. She has a squeaky voice, especially when she's excited . . ."

Helper: "Show me."

Boy: "Like this . . ." [Boy displays the characteristic mannerisms of his teacher, obviously having a good time doing it]

Helper: "Okay, I've got it now. Let's switch roles now. I'll be your teacher and you approach me just like you will do later."

Notice the choice of language the helper uses, stating casually that this confrontation *will* occur.

Boy: "Ah, Mrs. Skabernathy, I was, uh, wondering if maybe, ah, I could talk to you for a minute."

Helper: "I'm busy just now. Can't it wait until another time?"

Boy: [Looks at helper plaintively, as if to say: "What do I say now?"]

Helper: "Let's take a break for a second. Already you've gotten written off. You were so tentative in your approach that she didn't take you seriously."

Boy: "See, I told you she was mean."

Helper: "No, that's not what I said. If you approached her differently, you might get another kind of response."

Boy: "Yeah? Like what?"

Helper: "You be Mrs. Skabernathy, and I'll be you."

The helper is able to switch back and forth between playing the role of the antagonist and the consultant processing the episode. During impasses, it is easy enough for the helper to take on the role of the client, demonstrating new ways of dealing with the situation.

Obviously, role playing requires a degree of skill that isn't for the pure beginner or faint hearted. Nevertheless, the method is relatively straightforward. Whenever you sense that someone could profit from practicing some new skill or behavior, you stop talking about the matter and initiate some rehearsal. Most often, it is far better to do something rather than merely talk about it. Such a strategy might be indicated in the following circumstances:

- *Someone is feeling torn between two choices.* The client could be instructed to take turns articulating one side or the other, even switching chairs as he or she adopts that perspective.
- *When there is a confrontation that needs to take place.* Identify the antagonist, as well as any ancillary players involved. Act out the scenario, stopping periodically to offer support and feedback.
- *When there is unfinished business to be resolved.* With someone who feels lingering grief or guilt toward someone who died, or who even has many unexpressed thoughts and feelings toward that person, an "oral letter" could be initiated. You direct the client to begin a soliloquy, saying out loud all the things that have been left unsaid, while you act as scribe writing the verbalizations down in the form of a letter. This document can then be saved, edited, buried, or even ritually burned, symbolizing that the business has now been completed.
- *When it is apparent that the client isn't understanding what you're talking about.* Don't describe it; show it! You mention, for example, that the client might want to behave more assertively, rather than aggressively. It's clear from the client's face that he doesn't know the difference, so you spontaneously demonstrate the two styles by directing your wrath his way, then showing how you can say the same thing more effectively. Next, you could invite the client to try a round.

Although almost everyone could profit from some sort of behavioral rehearsal, role playing is not for every situation. Remember the general rule of not pressuring people to do things for which they don't feel ready.

Using Behavioral Interventions

There are a number of specialized techniques and interventions that are specifically designed to address behavioral problems such as phobias, chronic stress, situational anxiety, passivity, poor academic performance, boredom, addictions, and so on. Each of these methods requires training, practice, and supervision, but they are examples of the kinds of action-oriented, practical activities that can be made a part of helping efforts:

Autogenic training. This is a form of self-hypnosis that is taught to people who struggle with chronic stress. They learn to induce a trance state based on recordings you would customize for them. The object is to teach them greater self-control over their bodies, particularly with respect to breathing, muscle control, and concentration.

Relaxation training. This method is also used for reducing stress, dealing with insomnia, and improving all-around well-being. Clients are taught to systematically reduce the stress in each muscle group throughout the body.

Assertiveness training. This is an example of skill training for those who allow others to abuse their rights or who suffer emotional abuse. Clients are taught alternative ways of responding to conflict and how to stand up for themselves in socially appropriate ways.

Mindfulness. This group of techniques includes a whole host of meditative exercises (meditation, tai chi, yoga, and so on) that help people live more in the present moment. This can be helpful for reducing anxiety, depression, and boredom, as well as improving concentration and general well-being.

Homework. In this context, homework refers to specific tasks that people complete between sessions. Each assignment follows a theme or issue that was explored during the previous week and helps the person to put the ideas into action.

Giving Feedback

One thing that distinguishes helping encounters from other such relationships is the level of honesty and openness that is practiced. What often leads people to seek help (or be referred for it) is that they consistently engage in behavior that is self-defeating or annoying to others. They may have been told this in the past but could not hear what was said, perhaps because it was offered in ways that were too threatening. In part, your job is to tell people things that are difficult for them to hear, especially things that get them in trouble. To do this well, you must find a way to provide feedback that is not only accurate and useful but also that is well-timed and sensitively expressed. It is as if your client has been walking around most of his life with creamy garlic dressing on his chin, or spinach in his teeth, and doesn't seem to be aware that others can see it.

When offering feedback to clients about problematic behavior, keep the following principles in mind:

1. Be honest. It you have built a trusting relationship, then it is safe for you tell your client how he comes across—to you and perhaps to others.

    Helper: "I notice that you often interrupt me before I'm through speaking—just like you did right now. Every time you do that, it feels like you don't value what I'm saying, that . . . "

    Client: "That's not it at all. It's just . . ."

    Helper: "I notice that you are doing that again, right now."

    Client: "Oh."

2. Be as specific as you can. It is most useful if you can provide examples of what you are offering, especially if they occurred recently.

Helper: "You've complained that people don't take you seriously. I notice that you usually raise your voice at the end of every sentence, turning even statements into questions. That may be one reason why you are having trouble."

3. Try to be as concise and clear as you can. Don't use too many words, or people will find it hard to digest what you are saying.

4. Offer the feedback in the most caring and sensitive way you can. Remember that what you are saying may be perceived as frightening and threatening. Give the client a chance to process what was said and to respond. Yet it is a good idea to block attempts at defensiveness, as illustrated in the following example:

Helper: "Mickey, you complain that girls don't respond to you the way you want. Why do you think that is?"

Client: "You mean that I pick the wrong ones to approach?"

Helper: "That could be part of it. But I was thinking more about the way you present yourself."

Client: [With anger] "What do you mean?"

Helper: "You decide whether this fits or not. I notice that when you visit with me, your clothes are not always clean and it looks like you haven't shaved or showered."

Client: "I have too! It's just my look. If you weren't so out of touch . . ."

Helper: "I apologize. I am simply offering you what I observe in the hope that it might be useful to you. Obviously, you are doing something that is getting in your way. If it doesn't have anything to do with the first impressions you give, I wonder what that might be?"

As can be seen from this example, giving people feedback is often a difficult challenge, especially when they feel attacked. Yet when done with a certain diplomacy, such an intervention can be life changing. Feedback like this is almost always a part of the rehearsal and role-playing techniques previously described.

Using Imagery

Another kind of rehearsal takes place inside the person's mind. Fantasies, after all, can be a relatively nonthreatening way to help people imagine future possibilities. "Picture a time in the future," you might begin, "when you can finally do what you want." Then you set the scene more vividly: "Really imagine where you are and what you are doing. See yourself clearly as a person without fears and doubts. You are powerful and in control. Now, hold on to that image so you can return to it whenever you need it."

Visualizing the future is only one way to use imagery techniques to promote action. Here are a few others:

- *Imagery rehearsal.* Ask the client to picture herself in a stressful encounter that she dreads. Take her through a scenario in which you help her to review exactly what she will do and how she will do it.
- *Relaxation training.* As a form of stress reduction, instruct a client to imagine a scene that is especially soothing—lying on a beach, swinging in a hammock, walking through a meadow—whatever is most effective for that individual. Teach the person to go to this place in her head whenever she feels excessive pain, fear, or discomfort.
- *Guided imagery.* Act as the tour guide, and take the person on a fantasy trip that includes the features that you believe would be most helpful for the person at that moment. Sometimes, you may wish to work "metaphorically" when someone is especially anxious or resistant. For example, a client who has trouble getting out of bed and getting going in the morning can be led on a fantasy journey in which he sails along in the bed, watching the world around him, but he is unable to participate directly.
- *Inoculation.* Imagery can be used to counteract negative images, panic attacks, intense pain, or even disease processes. Cancer patients might be asked to imagine their immune system launching a counterattack against the "enemy invasion."

In any of these situations, imagery becomes a form of internal rehearsal in which people can harness the power of their own imaginations to motivate action. Through systematic practice, they develop new internal resources and skills for counteracting negative thinking, combating negative emotions, dealing with stress, handling disappointments, and developing more positive attitudes toward themselves and the world.

Dealing With Resistance

There is some debate as to whether people you are helping are actually being resistant or whether they are just cooperating in unusual ways. I am not really kidding. Even acknowledging that some of the people you try to help will be a giant pain in the butt—annoying, manipulative, controlling, seductive, or abusive—resistance is more a state of mind than circumstances. It is actually the client's "job" to act with you exactly as he or she would in the outside world. Because, by definition, this person is troubled and dysfunctional, it is only natural that you would encounter behavior that you (and others) find difficult. Remember, however, that is why you are consulting with the person in the first place.

Although I don't wish to minimize the frustration you will encounter when working with some individuals who are extraordinarily resistant to change and amazingly creative in getting underneath your skin, I do wish to point out that you can respond internally with a variety of reactions. You can belittle this person and call him or her names like "borderline," "crazy," or others that are even less flattering. You can blame this person for making your work so difficult. You can complain to others about how ungrateful and uncooperative the person is. Or, as an alternative, you can see this person as doing the best he can under the circumstances. If he could do anything else other than what he was doing, he would try it. This is all he can do for now, and you have to live with it as best you can.

That is not to say you should deny that resistance exists or tolerate acts of disrespect or manipulation. However, to sort out the best approach to take with someone who is not responding to your efforts, you will need to remain calm inside. You can't take what is going on personally, and you must not devalue or diminish the person just because you are feeling frustrated and helpless.

When encountering what you believe is resistance, try the following:

1. Remind yourself of the following: "This isn't personal," "She's doing the best she can," "This is the best he can do for now."

2. Stop whining and complaining just because the person is not meeting your expectations.

3. Stop working so hard. You may be overinvolved and trying too hard to make things happen. When what you are doing isn't working, try the opposite, that is, back off.

4. Get some help. Consult with others. If all else fails and you aren't doing the person, or yourself, much good, refer her elsewhere.

5. Give yourself permission to be more flexible and inventive in your approach. Your usual stuff isn't working, so it's time to try something completely different. This is the "gift" this person can offer you—encouragement to go beyond your own limits.

6. Set boundaries and limits. If you are feeling manipulated or abused, protect yourself by enforcing rules more consistently.

7. Examine the state of your relationship. Go back to basics to build mutual trust.

8. If working with the person individually isn't working, operate on a more systemic level. Invite members of the family to join you. Find out who has leverage and use that person's influence.

9. Focus not just on what isn't working but what has worked.

10. Keep your sense of humor. You are probably taking all this way too seriously. Lighten up.

Employing Adjuncts

Getting change moving might be the easy part; it is far more challenging to keep the momentum going. Once people take action in their lives, often the changes do not last very long. That is why you will need to devise ways that progress may continue without you present, long after your work is done.

The object of therapeutic adjuncts is to provide a structure for self-change to continue. Sometimes readings are assigned or books are recommended as a way to reinforce the concepts discussed in sessions. Watching movies that deal with relevant themes might also be a way for clients to participate vicariously in change processes that might parallel their own.

Perhaps most commonly, people are encouraged to keep journals to reflect on conversations, set goals for the future, and practice new behaviors (such as the suggestions in the previous chapter). As I mentioned previously, you might find such a vehicle useful in your own learning that is taking place. Imagine yourself writing every few days about the new insights you have realized, ideas you want to remember, and revelations that have become clear about your innermost thoughts and feelings. Picture, furthermore, that this journal could be used for you to practice some of the new skills you are learning—on yourself. Every new technique could be applied to some facet of your own life. You could process areas in which you feel some difficulty, work through points of confusion, and just talk to yourself about issues that arise.

Not only would keeping a journal help you to be accountable to yourself for future goals you have committed yourself to in writing, but it would nudge you to keep challenging yourself in new ways. These same advantages would be useful for those you are helping as well. They can be encouraged to monitor their own progress. Then, once your sessions are done, they will have a documented record of what they learned and how they made the progress they did.

Besides journaling, a number of other adjuncts might be employed in help-ing efforts. These can include seeing movies or reading fiction or nonfiction books that are relevant to a presenting problem. Those experiencing marital conflicts, relationship problems, addictions, or depression can be referred to specific sources that explore these issues in depth and may offer some con-structive guidance or support.

Support groups also prove useful for those who are attempting to make big changes in their lives. Most commonly, this is part of recovering from addictions, but it can include ongoing support for a host of issues related to physical problems, grief and loss, and other life adjustments.

When You Don't Have Enough Time

There is rarely enough time to do everything you want with those you try to help. The realities of your schedule and your clients' distractions often make it difficult to meet on a regular basis for very long. Sometimes, you are lucky if you can see someone more than a few times before the relationship ends pre-maturely. Nevertheless, even with limited time—even a single session or two—it is still possible to make significant progress. In the next chapter, we look at action strategies that are specifically designed to work in brief periods of time.

For Review

- Make certain that exploration has been completed before moving forward to action strategies.
- Resistance to change and to your helping efforts is normal and expected. This represents feedback to you that the person needs time and support to get through the struggle.
- Action strategies can be internally or externally based. Regardless of the plan implemented, it is essential to provide support, monitor progress, make adjust-ments as needed, and help the person generalize what was learned to other areas of life.
- You have lots of action strategies at your disposal—too many choices, actu-ally. Consult a supervisor or more experienced colleague when designing inter-ventions. Negotiate the plan with your client so it becomes a joint effort.

For Reflection and Practice

1. Meet in a group or with a few classmates, and talk to each other about a time when insight was not enough and when you needed to take decisive action to make lasting change. Look for common themes among your stories.

2. Reflect on a time in your life that you felt resistant to change that you knew was good for you. What were some of your fears and apprehensions? What helped you get through the reluctance you felt?

3. Think of something in your life that you have been avoiding or putting off. Devise an action strategy to help you complete the tasks. Commit yourself to follow through on your plan. Select someone you trust to become account-able to. Note what worked best for you. Consult with others if you feel stuck.

4. Work with a partner to identify some of your "self-talk" (internal dialogue) or irrational beliefs that lead to exaggerated emotional responses. Dispute those self-sabotaging thoughts by substituting others that are more reality based.

5. Get together with several classmates. Structure a role-play exercise that gets you all involved in acting out a scenario. Pick a situation that is more humor-ous than serious because you have little training and experience with this method (you do not want to hurt anyone).

6. Try relaxation training by listening to a tape or following a scripted program that can be found in many behavioral therapy texts. Practice using this method as a way of reducing your stress levels.

For Further Reading

Beck, J. (2005). *Cognitive therapy for challenging problems: What to do when the basics don't work.* New York: Guilford.

Egan, G. (2006). *Essentials of skilled helping: Managing problems, developing oppor-tunities.* Belmont, CA: Wadsworth.

Hutchinson, D. (2007). *The essential counselor: Process, skills, and techniques.* Boston: Lahaska Press.

Kabat-Zinn, J. (2005). *Coming to our senses: Healing ourselves and the world through mindfulness.* New York: Hyperion.

Kottler, J. A., & Chen, D. (2008). *Stress management and prevention: Applications to daily life.* Belmont, CA: Wadsworth.

Leahy, R. L. (2006). *Roadblocks in cognitive-behavioral therapy: Transforming chal-lenges into opportunities for change.* New York: Guilford.

McHenry, B., & McHenry, J. (2007). *What therapists say and why they say it: Effective therapeutic responses and techniques.* Boston: Pearson.

McKay, M., Wood, J. C., & Brantley, J. (2007). *Dialectical behavior therapy work-book: Practical DBT exercises for learning mindfulness, interpersonal effective-ness, emotional regulation, and distress tolerance.* Oakland, CA: New Harbinger.

Westbrook, D., Kennerley, H., & Kirk, J. (2007). *An introduction to cognitive behav-ior therapy: Skills and applications.* Thousand Oaks, CA: Sage.

7

Brief Interventions

A few decades ago it would have been considered sacrilegious, if not ridiculous, to consider providing significant assistance in a few sessions. Effective helping was supposed to take months, if not years. How could you possibly get to know someone, much less get a handle on his or her problems, without spending hundreds of hours together in conversation? Furthermore, everyone knows that refashioning one's life, reshaping one's personality, or initiating significant changes takes a very long time.

Then along came a few mavericks who suggested that perhaps permanent changes could happen much quicker if our efforts were more focused and strategic. The impetus for developing brief interventions came from several sources:

1. Family therapists, who discovered ways to promote changes in the system that people are part of by realigning the hierarchies of power

2. Problem-solving therapists, who devised innovative strategies for resolving specific symptoms without worrying too much about other issues

3. School counselors and crisis intervention specialists, who had to find ways to help people in just a few sessions

4. Administrators of managed care organizations, who demanded that health care professionals operate more efficiently and accountably

Some Cautionary Advice

Remember: the first principle of any helping effort is that even if you do not make things better, do not do anything that could make things worse. Many of the skills and strategies presented earlier are designed to initiate gradual, incremental changes at a pace that is manageable for clients. In this chapter, however, we will be examining some methods that are rather dramatic, intrusive, and forceful. Let me be very clear: They are not designed to be used by beginning helpers without considerable training and supervision.

Why then, you might ask, are brief methods included at all? That is a very good question indeed.

Quite simply, in our current times of increased accountability, public impatience, and managed care controls, helpers no longer have the luxury of taking their time to promote changes as part of an ongoing relationship that lasts many months. Often, we are called on to make a difference in a matter of weeks, or sometimes in a single session! As challenging as this might sound, there are, in fact, many new innovations and advances that make brief change not only possible, but likely, if certain strategies are pursued.

In this chapter, in particular, we are talking about a very sophisticated and powerful set of interventions that require close supervision from more experienced practitioners. Nevertheless, it is useful (perhaps even necessary) for you to understand the basics of brief interventions so that you can meet the needs of those who are in crisis or who do not have the time for lengthier treatment. Just keep in mind that even more than other strategies we have covered, you must receive considerable training and supervision to employ brief interventions safely.

Principles of Brief Intervention

There are currently dozens of different approaches to brief intervention, many of them abbreviated versions of longer term methods and others designed specifically for short-term treatment. Many of these methods might focus on different facets of change, but all share the following assumptions:

1. Change can take place very quickly if interventions are specific and targeted to particular goals.

2. Emphasis should be placed on the present rather than the past.

3. Contracts are developed that define specific objectives that will be attained in limited time parameters.

4. Helpers are highly active, directive, and innovative in their attempts to break dysfunctional patterns and establish new ones.

5. Approaches are highly flexible, experimental, and pragmatic in their means for solving problems.

6. Initiating little changes at first can lead to bigger changes later.

7. Attention is directed not only to what is wrong but also to what is working well.

It must also be emphasized that because these methods are so potent and fast acting, considerable training and supervision are required to make sure you don't hurt anyone. This is in marked contrast to the relatively benign exploration skills mentioned previously.

A Different Way of Thinking About Change

It used to be that real change was thought of taking place only when "depth" work was undertaken, examining underlying issues, historical background, and unconscious drives. Nowadays, we look at change taking place on different levels. We have already looked at how cognitive helpers attempt to change thinking, which then changes behavior. Likewise, some practitioners believe that if you can change attitudes, then the rest will follow, whereas others think that if you can change behavior, then attitudes will fall in line afterward. Still others ignore individual changes, believing instead that provoking systemic change is the most effective course of action. What all this means is that the business of change is very complicated. Nevertheless, there is some evidence to indicate that you can make a difference in someone's life, sometimes in a single contact, if you follow certain procedures.

With all brief helping efforts, you will still concentrate on developing an alliance that is based on trust, respect, and caring. You will still use all the skills you have learned thus far to communicate your understanding of the client's experience. One difference, however, is that you are likely to work on specific, attainable goals that can be reasonably accomplished in the time allotted.

An Abbreviated Process

You might recall from your own experiences how you made significant changes as a result of very limited contact with someone. Sometimes, it could be one thing that someone said that got through to you like nothing else had before. In other instances, it was less what was said than something else that got your attention in a major way.

In brief interventions, you will be concentrating on several sequential steps:

1. Find out what the problem is.

2. Focus primarily on this presenting complaint.

3. Find exceptions to the problem. Nobody is dysfunctional all the time. Discover those specific instances when the person did not lose control or experience difficulty.

4. Discover not only what has already worked, but what hasn't worked. There is no sense wasting your time trying things that have already been tested.

5. Because time is so limited, you must enforce boundaries to stay with the presenting problem; otherwise, you will end up distracted.

6. Develop interventions that are designed to shake things up and get the person moving. If one strategy doesn't work, try another, perhaps even the opposite of what you have already attempted.

7. Get the person to do something different. People remain stuck because they don't see choices. Your job is to stimulate new options.

Reframing Problems

The way you define the problem will determine whether you can help the person solve it. If someone comes in and says he is "shy" or "stupid" or "a failure," you have really got your work cut out for you, because you are facing major personality reconstruction. If, on the other hand, the problem is "reframed" as "I hold myself back in new social situations," "I pretend to act stupidly when I don't feel like working hard," or "I have occasionally not done as well as I wanted to," then you are faced with a quite-manageable series of challenges.

Reframing involves taking a problem that is presented in a way that makes it difficult to deal with and casting it in a distinctly different light. There is a real artistry to this skill, a talent that comes from practice. When you do it well, you will be amazed at how dramatically you can alter a situation that seemed hopeless before.

Notice in the following examples how different the original problem seems after it has been reframed.

Example 1

Presenting Problem: "I'm a troublemaker. Always been one. That's what my parents and teachers have always told me."

Reframed Problem: "You have a lot of energy and a playful spirit that sometimes gets you in trouble when you're bored."

The second definition certainly gives you a lot more room to maneuver if you want to help this person. Whereas it's very difficult and time consuming to change someone who has a personality disorder (troublemaker), it's not nearly as daunting to help someone channel energy more constructively.

Example 2

Presenting Problem: "My husband drinks too much and spends all our money. I try to get him to stop but there's no use. That's why I just gave up."

Reframed Problem: "You love your husband a lot and that's why you've stayed with him through some difficult times. Because you haven't been able to get him to stop his behavior, you are now ready to try some new things that might get through."

In this example, the problem is defined in a more positive frame, emphasizing the client's devotion rather than frustration. Also, focus has been placed on what can be done rather than on what hasn't worked.

When you become aware that you are feeling helpless or discouraged as you hear someone's story, that is a trigger that it's time to reframe the situation in a way that makes you both feel more empowered.

Look for Exceptions

When people are suffering, they tend to go on at length about their various complaints. They whine a lot. They talk about all the problems they have. Furthermore, they think that's what you want to hear about.

Indeed, you do need to know about what the problems are to have a hand in bringing them to some resolution. However, the side effect that comes from talking about what's wrong all the time is reinforcing the idea that things are looking grim.

Brief therapists of all persuasions routinely ask their clients a startling question: "I hear about all the troubles you've been having lately, but tell me, what are some things that are going well for you?"

I warn you: Most people will not cooperate with this inquiry. They would rather keep telling you about what has been going wrong than what has been right. Still, you must ask them again to concentrate on some exceptions to their misery. By doing so, you not only force people to lend greater balance to their situations, but you also remind them that they do, in fact, exercise some control over their predicaments. Nobody is a failure all the time. Occasionally, even by accident, things turn out okay. Whenever you can, try to bring attention to these exceptions, as illustrated in the following with a depressed girl who has all but given up:

Girl: "I don't see how it will ever get better. It's always been this way and probably always will."

You: "I noticed you said 'always,' as if there has never been a time when things have been any different."

Girl: "That's right."

You: "I know it must seem that way to you, but I'm curious: Think of a time recently when you weren't feeling depressed, even for a few minutes."

Girl: "I can't."

You: "There hasn't been a single moment in your life when you haven't been depressed? Even during the past week, you can't think of a single moment in which you weren't feeling absolutely miserable?"

Girl: "Well, maybe."

You: "You mean maybe you can think of a time this week when you weren't feeling depressed? Maybe you were actually feeling okay?"

Girl: "Sort of."

You: "Tell me about it."

This kind of laborious and persistent pushing is what it often takes to get people to admit that their symptoms don't always take over their lives. There are times when they are able to maintain some control, and these deserve considerable scrutiny. If you can help the person to figure out what he or she is doing during symptom-free periods, then you are on your way to finding a solution to the problem.

Find Out What Works

You can save a lot of time and aggravation by finding out what the person has already done that has been effective. Checking out exceptions will give you clues, but you can find other ideas by conducting a thorough inventory. I like to ask people to review for me all the things they have already tried to solve their problem. I make the list as exhaustive as possible and put each item on one side of a sheet of paper or the other, depending on its effect. Here is what one such list looks like for the woman described earlier with multiple sclerosis:

What Works	What Doesn't Work
Going to physical therapy	Trying to walk the dog and keep up
Taking time off when I'm tired	Taking naps in the middle of the day
Coming to counseling	Talking to my mother about things
Playing with my children	Staying home alone

Naturally, we were able to think of many more things that didn't work rather than those that did. That is why she was depressed. Still, it gave us a starting point to look at strategies she could adopt.

Miracle Question

This relatively simple technique is like an all-purpose, relatively foolproof secret weapon that elicits solutions to difficult problems. Start by asking the person to close his or her eyes, and use imagery to produce a state of relaxation. Deep breathing and other systematic muscle relaxation techniques can be employed.

If you don't already know how to do this, basically you follow a set of instructions that guide the person to a deeper state of progressive relaxation. You might ask the person to picture himself or herself in a peaceful place— lying on a beach or sitting in a favorite sanctuary. The subject is directed to concentrate on deep breathing and then to imagine various muscle groups— from the top of the head to the tip of the toes—slowing, relaxing, loosening, and stretching themselves like rubber bands.

"As you lie there on this perfect beach," you might whisper, "feel the sand between your toes and the warm sun on your body. Listen to the waves in the background. Feel all your tension draining away with each breath you take."

This relaxation method works so well that you can use it as well for a variety of other helping situations, such as when someone is anxious or stressed. Essentially, you are teaching the person how to induce a state of hypnotic relaxation at will. This is a condition not only well-suited for stress reduction, but also for being influenced.

Once the person is feeling relaxed, use guided imagery to take the person into the future: "I want you to imagine that when you open your eyes, all your problems have been solved by a miracle. You no longer feel troubled by what brought you for help. Now, what things do you notice first are different?"

After the person is able to articulate how life is different now that the problem has been solved, he or she is next asked: "So, tell me, how did you solve the problem? What did you do that made the greatest difference?"

Because this is a fantasy exercise in which the person has projected himself or herself in the future to a time when he or she no longer has the problem, the client will often suggest the solution to his or her own predicament: "Well, I stopped ruminating so much, over and over, about everything bad that happened to me. I ignored all that stuff. Then I cut off contact with my friends who were dragging me down. I stopped calling my parents so much every time I wanted to punish them. I started relying more on myself. Then I met someone new . . ."

Because this is a fantasy exercise, people often feel more free to articulate what they could do to improve their lives. Basically, people do know what is best for themselves even if they don't want to be held accountable. In an indirect way, this technique invites people to solve their own problems, as well as instills hope for the future.

A Single Session

There will be times when it may only be feasible to have a single contact with someone. What, you might legitimately wonder, can you possibly do to help someone in a single meeting? You would be surprised.

Think back on your own experiences throughout your life in which you had a single conversation or encounter with someone that forever changed your life. Granted, this is rare. But then again, most of these experiences were serendipitous rather than intentional. Imagine what could be done if, first of all, you believed you could truly make a difference in someone's life during one session. Second, what if you actually planned to initiate change during this one contact?

It certainly isn't ideal to attempt interventions in one session. You need time to get to know someone, to build rapport, to formulate a plan—and that is just to get started. You also need time to assess what occurred afterward and make adjustments to the program. Still, if all you have is one meeting, then you might as well make the best of things and do what you can in this limited format.

Step 1: Start Early

The actual helping can begin with the very first contact, whether it was a phone conversation to schedule an appointment or some other incidental contact. Find out what is going on, and get the person started on things before you ever get together.

Step 2: Communicate Hope

The placebo effect refers to how positive expectations can have a powerful influence on eventual outcomes. If you believe that what you are doing will be helpful, and if the client believes you as well, then you are much more likely to do some good.

Step 3: Define Very Limited Goals

Find out what the person is willing to change right now. Don't waste time getting into areas in which he or she may feel ambivalent or resistant.

Step 4: Check Out What Is Already Working

Even in limited contact, you still have time to look for exceptions to the problem.

Step 5: Devise a Plan

Collaborate on some action that will take place.

Step 6: Follow Up and Refer

Even though you may have only one formal contact with a client, you can still follow up by phone to see how things turned out. You are also responsible for ensuring that the person seeks additional help if needed.

The most important things to keep in mind when attempting a single meeting may seem contradictory. On the one hand, remember that you can only do so much in such a limited format, so keep your goals modest. On the other hand, the more ambitious your expectations, potentially, the more dramatic the results can be. Everything depends on the person's readiness and motivation to change. If you get to someone at the right moment, *anything* can happen.

Crisis Intervention

A drug overdose. A domestic dispute. A catastrophic incident. Acute grief. A suicide attempt. Post-traumatic stress reaction. A victim of abuse. There are just a few of the crisis situations that require immediate attention and intervention. You don't have a lot of time. You must take action. And there is a lot at stake.

The basics of crisis intervention are (a) to find out what is going on, (b) to assess the dangers and immediate risks, (c) to take steps to restore equilibrium, and (d) to then find out what happened and why. You will use the same skills you have learned throughout this book—asking questions, reflecting feelings and content, and so on. The main difference is that you must address the immediate situation before you can do anything else.

Calm Yourself Down First

During crisis situations, there is much you can do by presenting yourself in a calm, confident, and poised manner. Also, if you aren't thinking clearly and rationally, you aren't going to be much good to someone else.

Active Listening

Find out what is going on. Assess dangers and immediate risks. Establish a trusting relationship. Offer support.

Communicate Caring

Let the person know that he or she is not alone.

Check for Substances

Find out first if the person has taken any drugs or medications that may be causing or contributing to the symptoms.

Reduce Danger Immediately

If you determine that the person is in imminent danger or at risk of hurting someone else, you must take steps to protect others' safety. This may involve calling an ambulance or the police. It most likely will involve some decisive intervention.

Bolster Support

People end up in crisis because their support system isn't working for them. Find out what other support is available but currently not accessed. Who are the most stable family members and friends? Who can be relied on? What steps can be taken to stabilize the situation?

Problem Solving

Collaborate with the person in crisis to take care of immediate concerns. Contract with the person not to do anything harmful until help is available or until the next session.

Why Now?

If there is time, look at the meaning of the crisis at this moment. How is the crisis trying to get the person's attention? What function is it serving?

After the Crisis

Once the immediate situation is in control, take steps to ensure there will not be a relapse.

What Can Be Learned

This is often the most interesting part, even if there isn't always the luxury of figuring out what occurred. Help the person identify some object lesson from the experience so the crisis can be reframed as something constructive.

Choose Your Method Carefully

Not everyone is well-suited for brief interventions. Much depends on the severity and intensity of the presenting problem, as well as the person's motivation and needs. In spite of the pressure you might feel to operate efficiently, or the realities you face that make protracted treatment unlikely, you must also consider what is in a person's best interests.

When problems are acute and of relatively recent onset, when there seem to be the makings of a solid relationship, when the person is eager and motivated, and when specific goals can be defined and acted on, then brief methods may be indicated. If, on the other hand, the person is struggling with deeper, chronic issues, you may not be able to rush things along as quickly as you prefer. Remember that there are many people who present problems that have little to do with the real reasons they asked for help. They may be hungry for intimacy and understanding. They feel ambivalent about change. They need to understand who they are and where they are headed.

As with all interventions, how long your program lasts depends on what is needed. One of the first decisions you will make during an initial contact with someone is what sort of treatment is required. Is this a short-term or long-term case? Of course, one way you might proceed is by trying brief intervention first to see if that takes care of the problem. If more work is needed, then you can always structure something that addresses underlying issues.

For Review

- The future of the helping professions appears to be moving in a direction of quicker, more efficient, more potent interventions that can be measured.
- With brief interventions, you concentrate mostly on symptomatic complaints. If the person requires more supportive help or needs work on self-esteem and confidence issues, make plans for other help in a different context (support group, etc.).
- Brief interventions are guided by a problem-solving orientation in which you help the person develop alternative ways to face the situation. Often, this process takes place by shaking things up.
- Crisis intervention work is often the most satisfying helping work because you can make a difference in a relatively brief period of time. Also, acute problems have a better prognosis than chronic ones.

For Reflection and Practice

1. Either as a reflective exercise or with a partner, think of some repetitive pattern you are stuck in. Promise yourself not to repeat the same things. Develop a list of other alternatives. Experiment with your new strategies until you find a more effective strategy.

2. An "I'm" is a self-descriptor that implies a total judgment of yourself: "I'm shy" or "I'm not good at math." Think of some "I'ms" that you are prone to using to describe yourself. Now come up with some exceptions when this label does not fit. Reframe your self-descriptors into a more accurate assessment of your behavior.

3. Use the "miracle question" to imagine a time in the future in which you have reached your most desired goals. Either tell a friend or classmate, or write in your journal, about what you did to make that dream happen.

4. Interview some counselors or therapists who do brief therapy and crisis intervention work. Find out about the joys of their work, as well as the frustrations.

5. Watch some demonstration videos of brief intervention methods in action.

For Further Reading

De Jong, P., & Berg, I. K. (2008). *Interviewing for solutions* (3rd ed.). Belmont, CA: Thomson.

de Shazer, S., Dolan, Y. M., Korman, H., Trepper, T., McCollum, E., & Berg, I. K. (2007). *More than miracles: The state of the art of solution-focused brief therapy.* New York: Haworth.

Graziano, A. M. (Ed.). (2006). *Behavior therapy with children.* Somerset, NJ: Aldine.

Guterman, J. T. (2005). *Mastering the art of solution-focused counseling.* Alexandria, VA: American Counseling Association.

Kaduson, H. G., & Schaefer, C. E. (2006). *Short-term play therapy for children* (2nd ed.). New York: Guilford.

Lazarus, A. A. (2006). *Brief but comprehensive psychotherapy: The multimodal way.* New York: Springer.

Ledley, D. R., Heimberg, R. G., & Marx, B. P. (2005). *Making cognitive-behavioral therapy work: Clinical process for new practitioners.* New York: Guilford.

Nardone, G., & Portelli, C. (2005). *Knowing through changing: The evolution of brief strategic therapy.* New York: Crown.

O'Connell, B. (2005). *Solution-focused therapy.* Thousand Oaks, CA: Sage.

Presbury, J., Echterling, L. G., & McKee, J. E. (2007). *Beyond brief counseling and therapy: An integrative approach.* Upper Saddle River, NJ: Prentice Hall.

Talmon, M. (1990). *Single session therapy: Maximizing the effect of the first (and often only) therapeutic encounter.* San Francisco: Jossey-Bass.

8

Leading Groups

M any practitioners believe that the future of helping is found in group structures. Whether in the form of support groups, guidance groups, personal growth groups, or even groups in which everyone is related to one another (also known as family counseling), group work is just more efficient. You can reach more people with fewer resources in a shorter period of time than you can in individual sessions. Furthermore, group environments more closely simulate the situations that people struggle with in their lives.

If helping people one on one is challenging, then trying to do so with many people present is infinitely more complex. As with brief interventions in the previous chapter, it is first expected that you would become familiar with the basic helping skills before you would attempt to apply them to more challenging situations. Hopefully, you would log your first experiences as a group leader working with an experienced and expert coleader. In fact, this might be the best way of all to become proficient in helping skills because you have the opportunity to practice strategies under the tutelage of a veteran who can maintain safety for members and provide you with valuable feedback. This is also an excellent setting in which to observe, experience, and apply a variety of helping skills.

Differences Between Group and Individual Sessions

The biggest difference, of course, is the number of people in the room. In groups, participants get less individual attention. They also have less privacy, because there are many witnesses to what is said and confidentiality can't be guaranteed.

You use many of the same skills in groups that you would use in any other helping situation. You still use active listening, interpret and reflect what you hear and see, confront as needed, and do all the other things that work so well to promote insight and change. In addition, there are a number of specialized skills that capitalize on group dynamics and stages.

There is far more to pay attention to in groups. You have to monitor how everyone is doing in the room. You have to not only keep track of what is going on with the person who is speaking, but how everyone else is reacting to it. You have to keep all participants engaged in the process. You are teaching everyone else in the group (or family) how to be most helpful to the person receiving assistance at any moment. Then you are guiding the process in such a way to make sure that needed help is delivered. Needless to say, this takes more skill, training, and expertise than doing individual work.

Some Advantages and Disadvantages

Before you decide to delve into this area, consider that you might not have much of a choice. Group work is the delivery service of the future because it is so much more cost efficient: You can reach more people who need help. There are other advantages as well, notably the kind of support for change that is provided. People don't feel so alone knowing that others have similar problems. They feel a sense of belonging, that they are part of something bigger than themselves. They are able to learn skills for interpersonal success and actually try them out in the group. In addition, there are opportunities for vicarious learning. Even when someone isn't the focus of attention, he or she can still learn a lot by watching others work on issues.

The rehearsal strategies we examined earlier that are so important to promoting action are even more potent in group settings. People can practice confronting one another. They can role play scenarios more realistically with multiple parts involved. They can get lots of honest feedback from their peers on how they are perceived.

With these powerful therapeutic forces, there are also some disadvantages and contraindications to be considered. Some people aren't ready for a group format. They are too intimidated or reluctant to speak honestly in front of others. They may withdraw or feel coerced from peer pressure. Because people receive less attention, it is easier to hide and not deal with pressing issues. Some participants can even be lost in the shuffle.

As a group leader, you have less control and influence that you do with just a single individual. This means that one toxic person can sabotage the group or one individual who acts out consistently can hurt the degree of trust and cohesion that has been built. For these reasons, casualties can more easily occur than they could otherwise.

Rest assured that you can prevent many of these disadvantages and capitalize on the many strengths of this helping modality if you become well-trained and work under close supervision with someone experienced in group work and you don't pressure anyone to do anything when he or she doesn't feel ready.

Work With a Coleader

The best way to learn to lead groups is to work with someone who knows what he or she is doing and who is willing to mentor you along the way. Seek out someone who has a lot of experience leading groups, someone you think would be a good teacher, and volunteer to colead a group with him or her. This offers some distinct advantages to your development as a counselor, but also to the group participants. When two leaders are working in a synchronized, effective way, the group can become an even more potent atmosphere for change to occur.

When you work with a coleader, follow these basic rules:

1. Sit opposite one another so you can see one another and also different members.

2. Take responsibility for making sure that both of you share equal chores and participation.

3. Take turns scanning while the other is doing the work so you can cue non-verbal behavior and monitor members.

4. Take timeouts and talk across the group as a method to stay synchronized and confront members indirectly.

5. Play off each other's energy to keep things dynamic and exciting.

6. Don't fall into predictable roles (good cop, bad cop) but alternate the functions you serve.

7. Make a plan for what you might do in the session, then be prepared to throw it away and go with what is happening.

8. Debrief one another after the group by not only talking about the members but also giving one another feedback that contains both supportive and constructive elements.

Even if circumstances prevent you from enjoying the luxury of working with a coleader, you can still "deputize" various group members at times to work with you as partners. For example, a prolonged silence has been going on for several minutes in a group you are leading on your own. You aren't sure what to do about it because you don't know what it means—there are different kinds of silence that dictate different interventions. For example, the silence could indicate that people are confused, not understanding what you said. Other possibilities might include the silence as an expression of resistance or anger, or perhaps the members are just taking time to reflect on what they want to say. Depending on how you read the situation, your intervention would take different forms.

Rather than just jumping in, you decide to empower one member who ordinarily doesn't say much.

Leader: "Tia, I've been noticing that people don't have much to say right now."

Tia: [Looks down, hoping to escape notice, or at least be left alone]

Leader: "I was wondering if you could help me with this because I'm confused right now."

Tia: [Shrugs] "I guess so."

Leader: "It's just that this silence has been going on for a while and I'm not sure what to do, whether I should jump in, or just let it last a bit longer."

Tia: "I'm not sure either."

Leader: "Well, if you could just help me reason this through, we might figure out together where to go next."

Tia: "Okay."

Leader: "So, Tia, what do you think is going on? Is this a good silence, the kind where people are thinking about stuff, or a bad silence, where people are just sitting around as confused as I am?"

Tia: "Well, I don't know about the rest of them, but I was thinking about what was said earlier. I think eventually I might have even said something."

Leader: "That's interesting. What about the rest of the folks here? What do you think has been going on with them?"

Tia: "I don't know. Maybe we should ask them."

Leader: "Good idea!"

The leader could have reasoned this through on his own, but instead he decided to recruit one member to help him as a temporary coleader in this dialogue. The participants heard all this discussion, of course, so they were actually taking part in their own heads.

This decision about what to do at any moment in the group, whether to intervene, and if so, what to do, is the toughest part of leadership. If we put aside, temporarily, *what* you should do at various times, let's look at *when* you should do something.

When to Intervene in Groups

I think of this little bell ringing in my head every time certain situations come up in a group. I may not know what I should do, such as when silence occurs for a long time, but I know I have to do something. It is a time for intervention.

I would suggest that you wire some little bells in your brain as well, so that when you are leading a group, if any of the following situations arise (summarized in Table 8 1), you will know that it's time to intervene.

Stop Abusive Behavior or Hostility

Even if you don't help anyone, don't permit anyone to get hurt. You must have rules in your groups that are enforced consistently. Some of these might include forbidding the use of disrespectful language or being verbally abusive toward anyone. You can have a rule about no "put-downs." Regardless of the specific norms that are established, you must intervene decisively whenever someone is treating others in ways that are less than considerate. It's okay to be passionate, to be angry, and to be upset, but not at the expense of others' rights.

Cut Off Distractions or Digressions

People ramble a lot in groups. They take too long to say what they want. They are threatened by something going on and so seek a distraction. They don't know what you expect or want. Sometimes, they are just singularly ineffective in their interpersonal skills.

Table 8.1   When to Intervene in Groups

- Initiate check-in
- Build trust and cohesiveness
- Stop disrespect or hostility
- Enforce appropriate rules and norms
- Redirect focus
- Reflect feelings or content
- Provide feedback
- Cue member input
- Draw connections among members
- Correct irrational thinking
- Model appropriate behavior
- Empower participants
- Offer support as needed
- Reinforce helpful contributions
- Encourage constructive risk taking
- Provide structure when needed
- Stop complaining
- Confront inconsistencies
- Draw closure on a topic or session

If you don't intervene at these times, you will lose others in the group who will become bored and disengaged. Furthermore, you have an obligation to make sure people get feedback on how they come across to others. Whatever someone does in a group, he or she probably does outside as well. You must help that person get honest reactions as to how they are perceived.

Whenever possible, I prefer not to be the one who does the confronting. It's not that I don't mind the role, because it comes with the territory of being a leader, it's just that people tend to feel more censured and threatened when they hear something critical from an authority figure. For that reason, I prefer to get others to do the work for me whenever possible. I like to look around the group, notice someone who looks to be reacting the same way I am, and then cue them to offer the feedback.

Noe: ". . . so I was telling him that I just had to go there. Did I tell you guys the story before when I was homeless and . . . I did? Well, maybe you didn't hear this part . . ."

Leader: "Excuse me, Noe? I couldn't help but notice that while you were speaking, Trina was making a face."

Trina: "No, I wasn't!"

Leader: "Trina, I don't mean it was a bad thing. I just observed that while Noe was talking, you were looking really bored. You kept yawning and shutting your eyes."

Trina: "Well I can't help it! I was bored. I've heard this story so many times."

Leader: "Don't tell me, tell Noe." [Points to Noe]

Trina: "It's true, Noe. You just take so damn long to say what you want."

Noe: "I don't mean to. I just . . ."

Leader: "I hate to interrupt, but I was wondering, Trina, if you might approach this in a slightly different way. I'm noticing that Noe is feeling defensive and attacked, so he isn't going to hear you like this. Perhaps you could phrase what you have to say in a way that he could more easily hear you."

Trina: "I'm sorry, Noe. I don't want to hurt you at all. It's just that sometimes I tune you out. I don't listen to you. It would help me a lot if you would look at me, at all of us, when you talk. It seems like you don't even care whether we are here or not."

This type of intervention, in which the leader cues someone else to offer the feedback, isn't possible in individual sessions. Yet this sort of interaction is quite usual in a group. If he is so inclined, Noe can now hear additional feedback from others as well. It may be easy to write off what Trina says, but it's much harder if others feel the same way. Think how effective an incident like this can be for someone: People have been put off by Noe his whole life but nobody has ever told him why, at least in a way that he could hear.

Spice Up Boredom or Passivity

When you sense the energy is low or things have become predictable, you must do something to increase the level of engagement in the group. You may have to change directions or structure abruptly, abandoning the present course of action. In some cases, you will have to use your body, your voice, and your whole being to get things going. But you can't be complacent. You can't let things slide. If participants aren't fully engaged in what is going on, you can't help them.

Correct Irrational Thinking

Just as you would during individual consultations, help people challenge their dysfunctional thought patterns. You might, for example, intervene in the following instances:

- When someone says "I can't" rather than "I won't."
- When a member mentions some irrational belief like "It's not fair" or "This is terrible that I'm not getting what I want."
- When someone disowns responsibility, as in, "She just made me so mad that I couldn't do hardly anything at all."
- When somebody shows signs of being perfectionistic.
- When someone uses self-limiting language: "I'll never be able to get it right."

Among your other responsibilities, you are acting as a language coach, instructing group members in more effective ways to communicate with one another, as well as ways to talk to themselves inside their heads.

Reinforce Disclosures or Positive Values

When someone in the group does something that you think is helpful, is constructive, or contributes to the spirit you want to create, support that behavior. When you reinforce particular actions, you increase the likelihood they will occur more often in the future. This is the case not only with the person you are speaking to, but vicariously; the effect is generalized to everyone in the group.

What are specific behaviors you might be inclined to reinforce? Here is a list of possibilities:

- When someone shares something risky or vulnerable.
- When a member uses "I," speaking only for himself or herself rather than for others.
- When someone shows a high degree of caring and empathy for others.
- When a member confronts someone else in a diplomatic and sensitive way.
- When a person corrects himself or herself for using inappropriate language or self-limiting ideas.
- When someone reports having completed a goal or therapeutic task.
- When members initiate actions that build cohesion, trust, or intimacy.

Whenever group participants do or say things that contribute to the general welfare of others, you want to support that behavior as much as you can. It might sound something like this:

Renee: "I'd been having such a hard time lately, and it felt so good to finally do something that was good in my life."

Jose: "You know, Renee, I'm really proud of you. I don't think that I could have done as much as you did so quickly."

Leader: "Yes, Jose, you're right about that. Renee did show a lot of courage. I especially appreciate that you not only noticed, but chose to tell her how you felt. That hasn't been easy for you in the past."

In one single verbalization, the leader is able to reinforce Renee making progress, but also draw attention to Jose's contribution. Other members in attendance will notice this, if even unconsciously, and will more likely act in similar ways in the future.

Provide Structure as Needed

There will be times your group will struggle. When you see members floundering, you must ask yourself why you think this is taking place. Are members not clear about what is expected? Are they playing games with you or themselves? Have things just run their course and it's time for a new direction?

Depending on what you determine is at stake, you may need to jump in and offer some direction. At the very least, you will wish to interpret what you see happening and invite group members to introduce structure that is lacking.

Stop Complaining

Don't let people whine and complain too much. They will blame others for their problems. They will focus on those who are not in the group. They will talk about how miserable they are and how helpless they feel. There is a point at which such complaints, especially when chronic and continuous, lead more to increased helplessness rather than relief.

Some leaders make rules that you aren't allowed to talk about things you can't do anything about. Another rule might be to avoid focusing on outsiders, because you can't do anything about their behavior, only your own.

If you model this intervention, as in "I notice you are complaining again. I wonder how you might redirect your focus to your own behavior in this situation," then eventually other members will catch on and confront one another.

Comfort Someone Feeling Anxious

If you sense that someone is having a particularly hard time, you must take steps to offer comfort. You can either do this yourself, or even better, encourage others to do so. When a woman admitted, for the first time, that she had been sexually abused as a child, she broke into tears. You could tell she was feeling embarrassed by this emotional outburst, not to mention revealing her deepest secret. Other group members appeared nervous themselves, unsure how to respond. This is a critical moment in the group, clearly a time for some intervention.

Instead of being the one to tell her that you are proud of the risk she took in sharing the hidden part of herself, you notice another woman in the group who also seems to be on the verge of tears. You don't know if this is because she can relate to this issue because of a similar experience in her own past, or because she just feels empathy toward her peer:

Leader: "Cammie, when Liza was telling us about her abuse, you seemed to be feeling quite a lot yourself. What's going on?"

Cammie: "I don't know exactly. I just think that Liza . . ."

Leader: "Tell Liza."

Cammie: "Liza, I haven't had an experience like the horrible one you just described, but I do know what it's like to be used and then being made to feel guilty afterward."

Leader: "I notice some of the rest of you are nodding your heads, as if this is also something you can relate to. Tell Liza how you feel about what she shared."

Liza is not only being reinforced and supported for what she revealed, but greater cohesion and intimacy is being created in the group from her disclosure. In addition to any personal goals that each participant works on, this general feeling of intimacy and mutual trust is healing in and of itself.

Confront Inconsistencies

Just as you would do in individual sessions, when you see someone do or say something that is incongruent or inconsistent, bring attention to that discrepancy so people are held accountable for their behavior and can profit from hearing feedback. Once you model this behavior enough, other group members will get into the swing of things and confront one another as well.

Practical Considerations in Running a Group

You need to make several decisions about the kind of group you want to create and how you choose to lead it.

Group Composition

From a marketing standpoint, it is easier to "sell" a group when it has a particular theme—assertiveness training, grief support, parents without partners, problem solving, chronic illness, divorce adjustment, addiction recovery—there are hundreds of possibilities. People are more inclined to sign up for a group when they know that others will share their problems. This is conducive to developing trust and cohesion quicker.

Homogeneous groups have the advantage of shared issues but also the disadvantage that because everyone has the same problem, it's hard to help one another from a position of strength. When everyone in a group has problems of impulse control, how do they guide one another? Sometimes, they will even gang up on the leader as a way to protect themselves.

Heterogeneous groups, those that are as diverse as possible in age, background, and problems, may seem harder to manage but may in some ways be much easier to lead. For one thing, a diverse group more closely parallels the real world so there are more opportunities for realistic practice. Second, because people are there for a variety of reasons, they are in a greater position to help one another with issues they may have already resolved. One person may have trouble committing himself to relationships, but he is quite skilled at helping others overcome fears of failure. Another member is generally very shy and reticent, except when it comes to talking about ways she has overcome an eating disorder. In each case, members can operate from strengths as well as weaknesses.

Give some thought to what kind of group you want to create. Consider not only the composition of the group, but its structure and goals.

Working With a Coleader

If you are fortunate enough to work with a coleader, make sure you spend enough time together preparing how you will function as a team. There is nothing more divisive or destructive than having members participating in a group in which the two leaders are constantly at odds, undermining one another. It isn't necessary that you have the same approach—just that you demonstrate respect and collaboration in the ways you work together. It is also helpful if you function as equals in terms of power and contributions so that members don't perceive one leader as marginalized.

To help ensure that both leaders work in concert with one another, it is a good idea to sit on opposite sides of the circle. This makes it possible for you to observe and scan different members, while it also allows you both to watch one another closely for signals and cues. It is also a good idea to develop a signal system between you so that you can communicate during the session. At the very least, you would want a signal to indicate: "Time is almost up," "Let's move on," "I'm confused," and "Let's take a time-out."

It is perfectly acceptable to take a time-out in the group, during which the two of you can speak together openly about what is going on. This can even be especially helpful during times when you seem to be moving in different directions:

Leader 1:   "I wonder if we might pause for a moment?" [Indicates that she is speaking to her coleader across the room]

Leader 2:   "Sure. What's up?"

Leader 1:   "I'm just a little uncertain right now whether we should be continuing with Ida, who seems like she's had enough attention, or move on to Diego, who said he wanted some time today."

Leader 2:   "Why don't we finish up with Ida first, see what else she wants, and then we can move on?"

Leader 1:   "Sounds good."

This brief consultation, right in front of the group, allows members to make sure they are synchronized. Even when there is disagreement or conflict, members can find the time-out instructive because it models with the way that two "coparents" resolve their differences. The important thing is to keep these consultations brief.

Screening

It is generally a good idea to screen members before you admit them into the group. There are certain individuals who may not do well in such a setting, for example, those who are

- Characteristically shy, passive, and intimidated, as well as not inclined to express themselves in groups
- Manipulative, controlling, and deceitful
- Dominating and power hungry
- Severely disturbed in their cognitive functioning
- Hostile, angry, and inclined to act out
- Extremely negative in outlook or quite resistant to other perspectives

Group interactions require a degree of give and take. You want participants who will not pollute the process or infect other members with their negative attitudes or toxic interpersonal styles. When possible, you should have a screening interview with prospective participants to explain what you have in mind and determine if they will be a good match for your intentions. Even with such interviews, the likelihood that you could really screen out someone who is determined to get in (and so will lie and present himself or herself in the best possible light) is remote. This is why at times you may have to ask members to leave a group once it gets going if their behavior is consistently disruptive.

Ground Rules

You will either present the norms for your group or allow the participants to create them. You must come up with guidelines regarding acceptable and unacceptable behavior, as well as consequences for violating the rules. For example, you will need to agree on attendance policies—what happens to those who come late or miss sessions. You will need rules for acting in respectful ways. You will want to agree on rules for how someone leaves the group (must they give notice?) or how new members are added.

Beginning the Group

All groups go through a similar series of stages: a beginning, when norms are first established; a working stage, when people actually get into their stuff and work on their problems; then an ending stage. Devise a way to begin your groups so that people can get to know one another in an efficient period of time. Try to create bonds immediately so that people will feel committed to the process. Quite simply: The object of the first group session is to get people to come back for the second one. If you can't do that, you can't help anyone.

The first session must not only help people to get to know one another and to get started on norms, but also to commit themselves to specific goals they want to work on. Provide a structure for participants to get feedback from one another. Secure their commitment to return.

Working Stage

Depending on the kind of group you are leading, its theme and goals, you would follow a format in which you begin each sessions with a "check-in." Each member briefly shares what is going on that week, perhaps disclosing tasks completed and current problems in need of attention. This review can take anywhere from 5 to 20 minutes, depending on the number of participants, the amount of time you have (most groups run one to two hours), and the stuff going on in people's lives that week.

You will be monitoring carefully what people disclose, deciding which individuals seem in most immediate need of help. Next, you will ask participants to "bid" for time by simply asking who wants to work on something that week. In a high-functioning group, there will be far more stuff to work on than there is time available. You may need to coordinate the allocation of attention, as this example shows.

Leader: "Okay, so Bret, you say you only need a few minutes just to get some feedback on your latest strategy for dealing with your father. Nicole, you seem reluctant to ask for help today but it strikes me that you have some serious stuff going on in your life right now. Tanya and Mike, you both expressed a need for some time as well. So, who wants to go first?"

The session is now taken up with addressing each of these concerns, exploring what is going on and then deciding whether there is some action to be taken. All group members function as coleaders, under the guidance of the leader who is teaching them about ways to be most helpful.

Although this problem-focused group can be one type of structure, another might be more theme related. Either the leader will introduce a particular theme to explore for the session, or sometimes it will emerge from one member's disclosure. Issues might arise, for example, related to fears of rejection, intimacy, loss of control, self-defeating behavior, family meddling, loneliness, stress, substance abuse, risk taking, or other problems that evolve from one person's disclosure.

Ending Stage

People often feel ambivalent about a group ending. They are scared, of course: Maybe the changes won't last; maybe they will slide back to their old, dysfunctional ways. They are also feeling excited, hopefully, about the progress they have made. They are about to win their freedom.

While ending a group, you want to help people let go and move on in their lives. Otherwise, they will remain "groupies" forever, addicted to groups to maintain their progress. This might not necessarily be a bad thing, as participants in Alcoholics Anonymous and other support groups will attest. Still, if you can help people continue their momentum without dependence on a group, that is probably preferable.

As a group ends, people usually have unfinished business with one another to complete. You want to help them communicate messages left unsaid. Finally, you need to create a structure by which people can make commitments toward future goals. A summary of things to do when closing a group is found in Table 8.2.

Table 8.2   When Closing a Group

- Facilitate a summary of the experience, as individual members and as a shared experience.

- Help members disclose what was learned and gained from the group.

- Project into the future as a means to help members plan goals and follow up.

- Prevent and plan for relapses by talking about these realistic concerns.

- Identify unfinished business, and discuss how it can be worked on after the group ends.

- Deal with loss and grief issues related to the group ending.

- Build in follow-up and accountability procedures so that members continue their progress.

- Use a memorable closing ritual to bring things toward completion.

For Review

- Group work has potential to be more powerful, efficient, and reality based than individual sessions.
- Group work also has potential to do more harm because the helper has less control, members receive less attention, peer pressure and coercion are strong, and confidentiality cannot be easily enforced.
- Whenever possible, work with a coleader to provide better coverage and safety for members, as well as supervision and feedback for yourself.
- There are specific instances (see Table 8.1) when you must intervene to protect members, enforce appropriate norms, and promote constructive change.
- Speaking personally, doing groups is simply a lot of fun. There is tremendous energy, caring, and movement evident. No matter how many groups you do, and for how long you do them, they are always different.

For Reflection and Practice

1. Review the major groups that you have been part of throughout your life. What roles do you characteristically play?

2. Consider a time that you experienced positive, lasting change as a result of participation in a group. What occurred in the group that made the most difference to you?

3. Find a growth or support group that you can observe (Alcoholics or Narcotics Anonymous, a church group, etc.). Pay attention to the dynamics and processes that occur in the group that seem to be most helpful to people. If possible, talk to the participants about what they like most about their experiences.

4. Ask if you can sit in on a group that has a professionally trained leader. Better yet, volunteer to participate in such a group at a local counseling center on campus or in the community.

5. Meet with a group of classmates to complete a group trust-building activity (e.g., values clarification). After the exercise, discuss with one another the dynamics that emerged, the roles that each of you played, and turning points that seemed to facilitate or inhibit the group process and productivity.

For Further Reading

Corey, G. (2008). *Theory and practice of group counseling* (7th ed.). Belmont, CA: Wadsworth.
Donigian, J., & Malnati, R. (2005). *Systematic group therapy: A triadic model.* Belmont, CA: Wadsworth.

Gladding, S. (2008). *Group work: A counseling specialty* (5th ed.). Englewood Cliffs, NJ: Merrill.

Jacobs, E. E., Masson, R. L., & Harvill, R. (2005). *Group counseling: Strategies and skills* (5th ed.). Belmont, CA: Wadsworth.

Johnson, D. W., & Johnson, F. P. (2006). *Joining together: Group theory and group skills* (9th ed.) Boston: Allyn & Bacon.

Keene, M., & Erford, B. T. (2006). *Group activities: Fired up for performance.* Upper Saddle River, NJ: Prentice Hall.

Kottler, J. A., & Englar-Carlson, M. (2008). *Learning group leadership: An experiential approach.* Thousand Oaks, CA: Sage.

Shechtman, Z. (2006). *Group counseling and psychotherapy with children and adolescents: Theory, research, and practice.* Mahway, NJ: Lawrence Erlbaum.

Trotzer, J. P. (2006). *The counselor and the group* (4th ed.). New York: Routledge.

Yalom, I., & Leszcz, M. (2005). *The theory and practice of group psychotherapy* (5th ed.). New York: Basic Books.

9

Looking at Yourself

One of the privileges of learning helping skills is that they not only work well with people you are paid to help, but they are also useful in your personal life. In fact, it probably is not optional to apply what you have learned in this book to your own issues and relationships. To help others effectively, you must do all you can to remain as clear headed and neutral as you can. Furthermore, much of what you can do for people might have less to do with any specific techniques or skills than with who you are as a person.

Practicing What You Preach

When you can present yourself to others as someone who is kind, confident, and persuasive, then you are likely to be influential. When you can demonstrate in your own life the same attributes you want others to develop, you are far more likely to teach those values.

There is nothing that devalues helping professions more than to have its practitioners walking around like hypocrites, unable to practice in their own lives what they ask of others. If you want to help others be more fully functioning, then that means you should take a similar stand in your own life to address your own unresolved issues.

Consider the following questions, answering them in your head, if not writing them down in the space provided:

- What haunts you most?

- In what ways are you not fully functioning?

- What are some aspects of your lifestyle that are unhealthy?

- Which are your most dysfunctional relationships?

- How do you "medicate" yourself for excessive stress?

- What are the lies you tell yourself?

- What is it about your "secret self" that remains hidden?

- What are your greatest doubts and insecurities?

- How is all of this likely to affect your work with clients?

The more open, honest, transparent, and authentic you become with others, even when you risk sharing your most shameful parts, the closer they feel toward you. I don't know about you, but I happen to feel drawn to those who are willing to risk revealing themselves as most vulnerable. I end up respecting them more for knowing and acknowledging their weaknesses, especially if they appear motivated to work on the issues. What about you?

Making Helping a Lifestyle

You don't just act like a helper when your "meter is running." You can't just turn your compassion on and off, feeling helpful to people only when you are paid to do so. Neither can you survive very long as a helper if you don't learn to set clear boundaries between yourself and others; otherwise, you will become burned out very quickly.

Being a helper is a way of life, a way of looking at the world in which you are sensitive to nuances in human behavior, empathic toward others, and effective as a communicator. This not only makes you a skilled professional, but a better friend, parent, sibling, and human being. If you decide to commit yourself to this type of work, you will continue to work toward your own growth on a daily basis. You must do everything you can to broaden your base of experience and make yourself as worldly and wise as possible.

Ethical Issues

Like any set of skills, helping strategies make you both powerful and influential. After all, they are designed specifically to foster trust and change people. This power can be used for both altruistic as well as self-serving purposes. No doubt you have heard of instances in which helpers have exploited or taken advantage of others.

Moral responsibility and ethical obligation come with training as a professional helper. In general, the following are some of the ethical and legal issues that affect what helpers do.

Values

You will often face situations in which those you help have very different value systems than your own. Just consider how this may come up in sessions related to abortion, premarital sex, sexual orientation, religious convictions, illicit drug use, fidelity, personal responsibility, and so on. Your job is not to impose your values of what is right and wrong on others, but to help them find their own way. This is especially crucial when working with clients who come from different or unfamiliar cultural backgrounds.

Informed Consent

The people you help have a right to clear and accurate information about the risks associated with your treatment attempts, your credentials and qualifications, and what your helping efforts can and cannot do.

Privileged Communication

Depending on your state, your work setting, and your professional affiliation, you may or may not be guaranteed the right to keep conversations private and confidential. You must inform clients about what may or may not be revealed to others. All helpers are required to report to authorities any instances in which a person may be a danger to himself or herself or to others.

Records

If you keep written documentation of your client contacts, you must also inform clients who else may have access to the records. For instance, courts may demand records in custody cases or other legal proceedings. Managed care organizations may also have access to written documentation.

Malpractice

The legal system also becomes involved in those instances in which a helper has engaged in behavior that may be deemed incompetent or beyond the scope of practice. Most often, this takes place during "boundary violations," that is, when a helper takes advantage of a client or engages in "dual relationships," such as sexual improprieties.

Protection From Harm

All helpers, from teachers and nurses to therapists and doctors, are required to protect the rights of those who are being abused physically or psychologically. Most often this applies to minor children, but it could also apply to the aged.

Competence

You will need to be very careful not to exceed the scope of your training and qualifications. Just as if you are not a physician, you cannot prescribe medication, if you are not a licensed psychologist or a certified social worker, or a licensed counselor or family therapist, you may be limited in what you are allowed to do. Check with a supervisor, your organizational policies, and the state regulation board.

Ethical Codes

Each profession has its own ethical codes that guide professional conduct. In spite of differences in their specialties, most of these codes cover the areas previously mentioned. They are designed to protect the welfare of the public and of clients and to maintain professional integrity. You would be well advised to consult the ethical code that applies to your own discipline and, as a beginner, follow the guidelines scrupulously. When in doubt about any potential conflicts or areas of confusion, consult with a supervisor or more experienced colleague.

The intent of this discussion is not to frighten you unduly with all the things that can go wrong, but rather to help you understand the awesome responsibility that comes with being a helper. You do hold people's lives in your hands, so you want to be very careful to operate with utmost care.

Getting the Most From Supervision

A book such as this represents just the beginning of your preparation as a helper. These basic skills will get you started, but you will want to supplement this introduction with other training. Getting into counseling as a client will give you one valuable perspective. Taking other classes and attending workshops will certainly help as well. Most of what you will learn, however, will come from your supervision sessions with an experienced expert who will monitor your cases.

To get the most from supervision, you will want to work with individuals (if you have any say in the matter) who are not only highly competent but also accessible. You will be talking to them mostly about your mistakes and failures, so you must feel reasonably safe in this relationship. If this isn't the case, then you will end up bringing up issues that are safe and present you in the best possible light, but those that won't necessarily stretch you in ways you need to grow.

If it is safe to do so, talk to your supervisor about the personal issues that are triggered by your work (called *countertransference reactions*), as well as the technical problems that arise. In an ideal situation, you will feel comfortable talking about the areas in which you feel most confused and frustrated. You will ask questions about issues that puzzle you. You will take risks in ways that parallel what you ask of your clients.

Joys of Helping

Congratulations on choosing to work in some capacity as a helper! There is no job more fulfilling for a variety of reasons. If you have been looking for ways to feel useful and to really believe you are making a difference in the world, then helping offers a perfect opportunity to promote positive changes, a little at a time.

In doing this sort of work, you will enjoy many benefits, not the least of which is your own self-respect. You will feel a sense of potency and power in knowing and doing things that are conducive to promoting intimacy, wisdom, and serenity. You will have a lifelong excuse for being inquisitive and growth oriented. You will be challenged every day to confront your own unresolved issues. You will enjoy the excitement, intensity, and drama of being captivated by the stories you hear. Yet unlike television or movies, in which you sit as a passive audience, when you are helping people, you can actually play an important role in directing the plot as it unfolds. You will have the honor and privilege of being part of others' journeys, not just as a companion, but as a guide.

For Review

- Helping is as much a lifestyle as a job. You have the opportunity to be the kind of person you would want others to be.
- You must be reflective and vigilant about your own personal issues that may pollute or impede your professional effectiveness.
- Among the most difficult challenges you will face involve ethical, moral, and legal conflicts in which your own values may clash with those of your clients.

For Reflection and Practice

1. Meet with a group of classmates and talk about some of your personal attributes and life experiences that will be most helpful and most inhibiting in your work as a helper.

2. Reviewing the reflective questions in the text, there likely emerged a few points that touched you more deeply than others. Spend some time examining the ways your unresolved issues and vulnerable areas might affect your helping role. Talk about your concerns with others you trust.

3. Read the ethical codes of your intended profession as well as a few guidebooks on resolving ethical dilemmas.

4. Get together with a group of classmates and talk to one another about the ethical conflicts you fear the most. Role play a few of the scenarios that have the most universal concerns (for example, a client who becomes seductive or who appears suicidal). Come to some consensus about appropriate actions that should be taken. Consult with your instructor and other experts about unresolved issues.

5. Interview helpers in the field about the most challenging ethical conflicts they have faced. Find out how they dealt with the problems, both internally and with others. Solicit their advice on how you could best prepare yourself to function ethically and morally as a helper.

6. Write a letter or journal entry to yourself in which you list the most significant things you learned throughout the course. Remind yourself about commitments you are prepared to make that will propel your helper training to the highest level of excellence.

For Further Reading

Frankl, V. E. (1992). *Man's search for meaning* (4th ed.). Boston: Beacon Press.

Gelson, C., & Hayes, J. (2007). *Countertransference and the therapist's inner experience: Perils and possibilities.* New York: Lawrence Erlbaum.

Kottler, J. A., & Carlson, J. (2005). *The client who changed me.* New York: Routledge.

Pope, K. S., & Vasquez, M. (2007). *Ethics in psychotherapy and counseling: A practical guide.* San Francisco: Jossey-Bass.

Remley, T. P., & Herlihy, B. (2007). *Ethical, legal, and professional issues in counseling* (2nd ed.) Upper Saddle River, NJ: Prentice Hall.

Robertiello, R. C., & Schoenewolf, G. (1987). *101 common therapeutic blunders.* Northvale, NJ: Jason Aronson.

Weiss, L. (2004). *Therapist's guide to self-care.* New York: Routledge.

Wishnie, H. A. (2005). *Working in the countertransference: Necessary entanglements.* New York: Jason Aronson.

Index

About the Author

Jeffrey A. Kottler is the author of more than 65 books in the fields of counseling, psychology, and education that have been translated into more than a dozen languages. His best known works include *Compassionate Therapy: Working With Difficult Clients, On Being a Therapist, Making Changes Last, Bad Therapy: Master Therapists Share Their Worst Failures, The Mummy at the Dining Room Table, Divine Madness: Ten Stories of Creative Struggle,* and *The Client Who Changed Me: Stories of Therapist Personal Transformation.* In addition to this primer, he has coauthored a more detailed skills text for Sage that explores each of the helping procedures in greater depth: *Applied Helping Skills: Transforming Lives.*

Jeffrey is professor and chair of the Department of Counseling at California State University, Fullerton. He is also cofounder of the Madhav Ghimire Foundation, which is devoted to helping marginalized and neglected children in Nepal.